D0254722

THE
TITANIC
STORY

DATE DUE

THE
TITANIC
STORY

HARD CHOICES, DANGEROUS DECISIONS

STEPHEN COX

OPEN COURT
Chicago and La Salle, Illinois

To order books from Open Court, call toll-free 1-800-815-2280.

Front cover illustration, from the painting, "Iceberg Right Ahead," courtesy of the artist, S.W. Fisher.

Open Court Publishing Company is a division of Carus Publishing Company.

First printing 1999

Printed and bound in the United States of America

Library of Congress Cataloging-in-Publication Data

Cox, Stephen, 1948–
    The Titanic story : hard choices, dangerous decisions / Stephen Cox.
       p. cm.
    Includes bibliographical references and index.
    ISBN 0-8126-9396-5 (pbk. : alk. paper)
    1. Titanic (Steamship)—History. 2. Shipwrecks—North Atlantic Ocean—History. I. Title.
G530.T6C69   1999
910'.91634—dc21
                                       99-19025
                                         CIP

For Norma Staver

Contents

Illustrations

Acknowledgments

R.W. Bradford published an early version of my thoughts about the *Titanic* in the May, 1997, issue of *Liberty,* not minding that it was much too long for a journal article—though it was much too short for a book. When I decided to make it into one, Andrea Millen Rich helped me find a superb editor, David Ramsay Steele of Open Court. David's support and advice were just what the project needed. Philip Armstrong of the Ulster Titanic Society (P.O. Box 401, Carrickfergus, Co. Antrim, Northern Ireland BT38 8US, U.K.; mgy@uts.dnet.co.uk) gave me encouragement and expert criticism. Claudia Jew of the Mariners' Museum in Newport News provided truly collegial help with photographs. Mark Taylor of the library at the University of California, San Diego, searched cunningly for rare books. Muriel Beroza helped me with Swedish research material. Ann Ramirez and Pam Clark solved my problems with hardware and software. Lawrence Waddy shared his understanding of human situations and his memories of war at sea. Garrett Brown, who always wants me to write and publish, whether I want to or not, helped in every way I let him. John Nelson took me to Mexico to see the big *Titanic* model. The project began and ended in conversations with Paul Beroza, who feels as I do about the *Titanic* story.

The Great Story

The story of the *Titanic* has been told before, and it will be told again. It is inexhaustible. We return to it over and over, as if we had missed something that we needed to find—either the truth of the event or its mystery.

This determination to revisit the *Titanic* is a curious cultural phenomenon. If knowing something means possessing a certain quantity of information about it, then the *Titanic* disaster is already one of the best known incidents in human history. Many people have devoted many years of their lives to investigating what happened aboard the *Titanic* on the night of April 14–15, 1912. Although they are far from having discovered all the facts, they know a great many more of them than any actual participant could possibly have known. Investigation continues; this book is part of it. But almost everybody knows at least the outlines of the story, and everybody knows its end. We heard it in childhood, when someone first told us that the *Titanic* was a giant ship that crashed into an iceberg, and most of the people died. So the surprise is gone; it was gone from the first.

Or is it? We may know how the story ends, but there is still something that we want to understand, some experience of life that we want to have. It has frequently been said that people are attracted to the *Titanic* story because it gives them the chance to imagine what they would have done if they had played a part

1. The beautiful *Titanic*. *Courtesy of the Mariners' Museum, Newport News, Virginia.*

in it, if they had built the ship, or sailed her, or faced death when she struck the iceberg. To try to imagine this is to begin retelling a story that is filled with excitement and adventure, with the secrets of other people's lives and other people's choices, and with the secrets that we discover about ourselves when we try to enact the lives of other people. We understand instinctively that the choices in the *Titanic* story were not easy. We understand that there are answers we do not have, mysteries we have not penetrated, human problems that cannot be solved even by nine decades of investigation. That is the reality.

But as T.S. Eliot wrote, "human kind cannot bear very much reality."[1] It is easier for us to contemplate the event, and our imagined roles in it, if we remove the psychological and moral mysteries and simplify the problems of choice, thereby constructing a narrative that is not very much about the *Titanic*, after all. And that, unfortunately, is how the *Titanic* story often gets told. It is told as if all the important issues were easy to resolve.

Most versions of the story, indeed, make it very obvious what we ourselves would have done if we had been involved—supposing that we had any common sense, or sense of right and wrong. It is all quite clear. If we had operated the *Titanic*, so it is suggested, we would certainly have taken the trouble to determine just how far from "unsinkable" she really was. We would have provided her with every conceivable safety device and mechanism of escape. We would have anticipated every hazard she might conceivably have encountered. We would have stopped her engines at the first sign of any danger. If, despite our precautions, something, somehow, had still happened to go wrong, we would have met the emergency in precisely the right way. We would have known precisely who should be allowed to enter a lifeboat, and in what order they should enter. No matter what role we played on the *Titanic*, we would have known everything there was to know about our duties to other people and (perhaps) ourselves. We would have calculated every individual's degree of moral responsibility to the twentieth decimal place.

And, speaking of moral responsibility, we would probably have been extremely reluctant to have anything to do with the *Titanic* to begin with. We would have understood that so immense, so costly, so arrogant an expression of technological self-confidence would immediately attract the vengeance of the gods, or God, or sheer blind fate.

We think we know these things, because we know the turn the story takes midway through the *Titanic*'s maiden voyage. From the perspective provided by that disastrous climax, the answers to all the big questions in the story can seem unmistakably evident—as if this were a story of certainties, not a story of risks. But when we start to believe that, we are drifting away from everything that makes the story a challenge to the imagination. We may drift so far that we lose the story.

A striking example of drifting away is the world's most expensive attempt at story-telling, the 1997 film *Titanic*. The film appears to start with the assumption that after many years of telling and retelling, one particular version of the story has made itself known and accepted by all, with no need for further thought. That version is certain and definite. It confidently identifies the cause of the disaster as the arrogance and incompetence of the type of people who built the ship and ran it, the type of people who luxuriated in the *Titanic*'s first-class accommodations, indulging a childish faith in the indestructibility of their technological toy and caring nothing whatever about anyone who might be hurt by it.

This view of things is convenient, in a way, because it allows for a radical simplification of the story. Like the passengers on the original vessel, passengers on the celluloid *Titanic* are neatly divided into classes and given treatment that is better or worse according to their class. But the new class system has a distinct advantage over the old. There is now no need to worry, as people in 1912 were prone to worry, about the possibility that *moral* status may have little or nothing to do with *social* status. The movie clarifies the relationship. It suggests that if you have money, then you are very probably deficient in morality; and if you have morality, you are very probably low on cash.

A first-class ticket for the 1997 voyage is good evidence that its possessor is terminally weak and silly, or perhaps just criminally insane—in any event, that he or she is the kind of person who would wantonly build such a ship as the *Titanic*, and then wantonly destroy it. By contrast, a passenger with a third-class ticket is quite likely to be strong, candid, irrepressibly vital, and (when necessity arises) wonderfully brave and clever. On the original *Titanic*, there was room for second-class travelers; on the new ship, there is no mediating space, no ambiguity; there are only moral aristocrats and moral bankrupts. We know these people; we have seen them in other movies. Their character, like their fate, is fixed.

Few people who were part of the *Titanic* story in 1912 are included in 1997's distant approximation of it. They were, apparently, too complicated and unpredictable, too risky to deal with. Some of their names were preserved, to maintain a nostalgic connection with actual life, but their identities were replaced by stereotypes. Yet without the *Titanic*'s troublesome real people, where is the substance of the *Titanic* story? What can replace them as a reason for telling it?

One of the film-makers' attempts at replacement is the ship itself—in literal terms, an 800-foot model of the ship, majestically recumbent on a desert beach in Baja California, where the film was shot, but capable of doing many impressive things when it goes "to sea." At times, one almost mistakes the imitation for the fact, such is the power of technology, even when it is used to rebuke the arrogance of technology, and such is our willingness to embark on any ship that is named *Titanic*, even if it is just a model.

But technology alone can never provide the sense of dramatic possibility, the special sense of adventure, that draws us to the *Titanic* story. The real *Titanic* was a marvellous technical accomplishment, but if she had not met with a fatal misfortune, she would soon have been superseded by other feats of technology. Within 20 years or so, the marvellous ship would have been sold for scrap; only maritime historians would remember her now. If she had perished in some disaster other than the one that overtook her, some catastrophe that lacked the sharp and solemn human drama of the incident we know, she would be remembered only as one more episode in the age-long conflict between naval architecture and the North Atlantic Ocean.

It is the drama of human choices that makes her story what it is. The film-makers freed themselves from the difficulties of that drama when they dispensed, by and large, with its characters. But they still needed to find a story about people, a story that would somehow evoke the memorable qualities of the original, human story.

Their way of finding it was to invent two attractive young people, a boy and a girl who fall in love for the first time on the decks of the *Titanic*. This invention has its assets and advantages; but it has one considerable disadvantage: it has nothing much to do with the *Titanic* story. The romance could occur at any time or place; it just happens to occur on a ship. The *Titanic* contributes the physical dangers that the romantic plot requires, but it is hard to see what the plot contributes to the *Titanic*. The new story poses none of the challenges of the old. There is now only one important question—Should we fall in love?—a question to which nearly everyone would answer Yes. The crisis of the real *Titanic* raised questions that were, and are, much less easily answered, questions to which, in many cases, no sure answers have been found.

Many of these questions are associated with profound moral problems, perennial issues of duty and responsibility that on the *Titanic* were rendered supernormally intense by the dramatic insistence that they all be decided *now*. Even the question of what the *Titanic* should have done at the moment when her lookouts sighted the iceberg ("right ahead!") is full of strange practical and moral risks.

The obvious answer, the answer that almost anyone's nerves would instantaneously signal, is, "Turn! Turn! Try not to hit it!" That was how the officer in charge on *Titanic*'s bridge responded when the lookouts phoned their warning from the crow's nest. First Officer William Murdoch did not hesitate. He turned the ship. He almost missed the iceberg. The *Titanic* almost got away. When she struck, the impact seemed slight. No one was killed. Many people continued sleeping. Few others could believe that anything had gone seriously wrong as the result of Murdoch's choice.

But something had gone wrong, and (according to one possible interpretation of reality) Murdoch's decision was responsible. Few ships' officers are trained to steer directly into icebergs, but in Murdoch's situation, at Murdoch's particular moment of risk and peril, it might have been far, far better if his response had been: "Aim for it! Try for a head-on crash!" As I will show in chapter 6, Murdoch had cause to believe that a modern ship would not be fatally damaged if it struck an iceberg head-on. If he had acted on that knowledge, the *Titanic* would likely have survived, and so would William Murdoch—instead of dying, as he did, in the disaster of that night, a heroic victim of his own decision.

Who will assume the responsibility of blaming him for his failure to make an apparently preposterous choice—even though it would have been much more heroic than the choice he actually made, simply because it would have appeared preposterous to everyone else? But who will assume the responsibility of saying that we should judge the moral significance of a decision without giving any consideration to its practical effects—even if one of those effects is the sinking of an ocean liner?

The Book of Common Prayer speaks of "the changes and chances of this life"; professional economists talk about "unavoidable risks"; professional gamblers mutter that "there's no such thing as a sure bet." All of them are right. Even true love, as the story of Romeo and Juliet informs us, represents an assumption of risks. Much greater than the risk of romantic love is the risk of deciding the fate of a mammoth ship with 2,200 people aboard. And within each of those people's lives there were innumerable risks, innumerable decisions.

William Murdoch was, for the moment, in charge of the *Titanic*. Other people were in charge of nothing more than the decision of whether or not to enter a lifeboat. Yet their choices might be a great deal more complicated than his. Do I have a right (they might ask themselves) to take a seat in a lifeboat, if I can do so without denying anyone else a seat? And what if someone *is* denied a seat? In that case, does it make any difference whether I am male or female, married or single, rich or poor, prominent or obscure? Do I have an obligation to help anyone else? If I do, how should I go about it? Do I know that I can do it effectively, or will my efforts, in some perversely unlucky way, manage to make things worse? If I try to help, how hard must I try? And how long do I have to decide? Will the answers start to look clearer and clearer as the water comes closer and closer? What do I know, and what should I do? Because I *must* do *something*.

Here is the heart of the real *Titanic* story; here are the changes and chances of this life in their full complexity.

In every episode of the story—the building of the ship and its navigation, its collision with the iceberg, the efforts to save its passengers, the continuing efforts to find and assess the truth about all these events—we confront the mysterious necessities of choice and risk. The choices and the risks are not just practical; they are moral, too. We are concerned with what was done, and what might have been done, but we are also concerned with what ought to have been done. When we retell the *Titanic* story, casting ourselves in the various roles available, we are trying (among other things) to judge, as best we can, the values that determined the characters' decisions. When we assume the risk of judging their values, we also assume the risk of judging our own.

This is a compelling drama, and a disturbing one. We feel its force most strongly when we enter it most deeply, when we look as closely as we can at what actually happened to individual people as they faced their mysterious moments of conflict and decision. Each of those moments is a collision point between several possible realities: what was done, with its known results; what might have been done (for, perhaps, equally good reasons), with all the results that this might have had; things known, and things surmised, and the moral reasoning that endeavors to understand it all.

2. *Titanic* emerges from the shipyard. *Courtesy of the Mariners' Museum, Newport News, Virginia.*

To journey with the *Titanic* is to journey across a sea of mysteries, to "steer," in Walt Whitman's phrase, "for the deep waters only." It is a morally perilous journey, and the reward is uncertain. When we arrive, if we ever do, at the end of the voyage, we may find that our view of life has been changed; in what way, we may not be able to estimate precisely. Perhaps, as Whitman suggests, the purpose of embarking on a journey like this is to encounter all the wreckage of past decisions and still be able to see, with the mind's eye, "one flag above all the rest,"

> emblem of man elate above death,
> Token of all brave captains and all intrepid sailors and mates,
> And all that went down doing their duty[2]

—or survived, believing that they, too, had managed to face the risks.

Choose anyone who traveled on the *Titanic*. Investigate that person's story. Soon you will discover that you have started on a greater voyage. . . .

"There Is No Time to Waste"

TIME: 1:40 A.M., Monday, April 15, 1912.
PLACE: The deck of a steamship lying motionless in the
        North Atlantic. The sky above is gaudy with stars,
        like the arch of an enormous stage.
ACTION: A man is looking at a lifeboat. He is making a
        decision.

What this man decides will strike many people as a very unpleasant surprise. It will make him as hated and reviled as any private figure of his generation. It will be studied by the investigative commissions of two great nations. It will be reproduced, and distorted, by every medium of popular information and entertainment. And it will remain—like thousands of other decisions that were made that night—a subject of seemingly endless controversy, an emblem of the mysteries that surround moral judgments.

The ship was the White Star liner *Titanic*. The man was J. Bruce Ismay, Managing Director of the White Star line. If you want to try making sense of the *Titanic* disaster, and of the countless other attempts to make sense of it, you can start with the comparatively simple story of J. Bruce Ismay.

3. Joseph Bruce Ismay, looking his best for the studio photographer—
handsome, cultured, confident. The picture was taken at some time
during the good days of his career, after the death of his father in 1899
and before the sinking of the *Titanic* in 1912. *Courtesy of the Mariners'*
Museum, Newport News, Virginia.

Ismay's life was inseparable from that of the White Star line. In 1867, when he was five years old, his father Thomas, a self-made capitalist, bought White Star in a liquidation sale. It was just a name and a flag; there were no ships attached; but he built it into the symbol and the reality of modern progress—a fleet of great steamships providing fast, dependable, and comfortable service between England and America.

Thomas Ismay was a hard man. When he left his house (a work of pigheaded ostentation that was staffed by 32 servants but possessed neither central heating nor modern bathtubs), he would place a stone on any fallen leaf that defaced the grounds. If the leaf remained in place when he returned, he would assemble his ten gardeners and "demand to know what they had been doing all day." [3]

Bullied and occasionally humiliated by his father, Bruce Ismay developed into a cranky, psychologically isolated adult. He was tall, well-built, well-dressed; but he was shy and self-defensively arrogant, full of inhibitions and inabilities. He would not speak in public (his father had enjoyed public speaking). He would not ride a horse (he had once accidentally ruined his father's horse). He would not drive a car, and he would not give advice to his chauffeur, because, he believed, the chauffeur "is in charge, and if he thinks we should go so fast it is not for me to interfere." [4]

Bruce Ismay was capable of doing mysterious things. One day, while he was riding back and forth on top of a streetcar (it was something he did when he needed to think), he saw a group of children playing on the roof of a building. He directed an assistant to find out what the building was. Told that it was an orphanage, Ismay immediately sent the management a check for the contemporary equivalent of $25,000. But even a sympathetic writer observes that Ismay "frightened" some of the people whom he actually knew: "He was full of destructive criticism. . . . He was dogmatic when asked for advice, which he gave readily, but having given it, he dismissed the subject and brooked no argument." [5]

A WORLD'S RECORD. ONE THIRD OF A MILE OF IRON & STEEL IN TWO SHIPS.
THE NEW WHITE STAR LINERS "OLYMPIC" & "TITANIC" AT BELFAST.

4. "Behold now behemoth, which I made with thee": *Olympic*, under repair, with her sister *Titanic*, under construction, at the Harland and Wolff shipyard in Belfast. A jubilant postcard of the time. *Courtesy of the Mariners' Museum, Newport News, Virginia.*

Thomas Ismay died in 1899. Three years later, Bruce Ismay arranged the sale of White Star to J.P. Morgan and his associates, retaining a managerial role but surrendering ultimate financial responsibility. Morgan was trying to monopolize North Atlantic shipping. His effort failed; the French line and the mighty Cunard line remained outside his grasp. But Ismay had a plan for improved competition. White Star would not try to rival the speed of Cunard's liners; it would build somewhat slower ships, but they would be larger and more attractive.

Three huge sister ships were born: *Olympic, Titanic,* and *Britannic. Olympic,* the first to be completed, began service in 1911. She was destined for many adventures. During World War I she was attacked four times by German submarines. In the final incident, she first evaded a torpedo, then rammed the attacking submarine and sank it. After that, she was known as "Old Reliable." In a less creditable engagement of 1934, she accidentally collided with the Nantucket Light Ship and sank that, too. She was retired from service in 1935 and died peacefully in a scrap yard. The third ship, *Britannic,* did not survive the first world war. Begun in late 1911 but not yet ready for passenger service when hostilities started, she was converted into a hospital ship. In November, 1916, she was sailing to an Aegean port to pick up patients when she hit a mine, exploded, and sank. She was the most considerable wartime loss of the British merchant marine.[6]

But the great story is *Titanic's.* Like her sisters, she was built at the Harland and Wolff shipyards in Belfast, Northern Ireland. On May 31, 1911, two days after the *Olympic* took to sea for the first time, the *Titanic* was launched amid the explosion of rockets, the cheering of 100,000 spectators, and the fluttering of signal flags spelling out the word "SUCCESS." It was the moment of Ismay's triumph. The *Titanic* was the largest moving object ever constructed. Her length was 883 feet, her beam was 93 feet, her gross tonnage was 46,000. She measured 58 feet from her boat deck (the location of her lifeboats, bridge, officers' quarters, and wireless station) down through decks A-F to the waterline (G deck: post office, handball court,

5. *Titanic* as a mountain of steel, assembled by thousands of workmen, piece by piece. She is not yet the "creature of cleaving wing." ("Titanic" in white letters on the bow appears to be an emphasis added by a later hand.) *Harland and Wolff Photographic Collection, © National Museums and Galleries of Northern Ireland, Ulster Folk and Transport Museum, H1561a.*

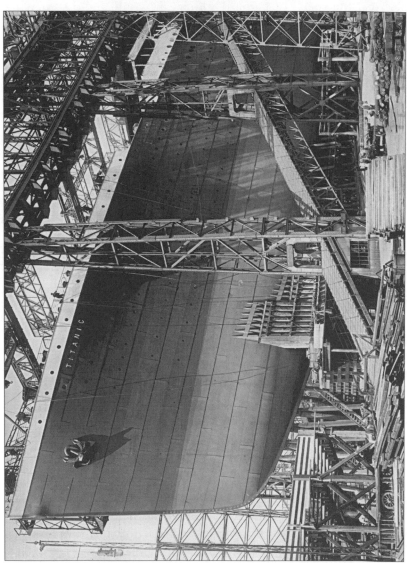

6. "We know what master laid thy keel": Ismay (right) and Lord Pirrie, senior partner of Harland and Wolff, inspecting the *Titanic* before her launch. The ship is thought to have been conceived in an after-dinner conversation between Ismay and Lord Pirrie in 1907. *Harland and Wolff Photographic Collection,* © *National Museums and Galleries of Northern Ireland, Ulster Folk and Transport Museum, 23640.*

baggage room, third-class passengers' quarters). Between the waterline and the keel (distance, another 35 feet) were the big iron rooms where hundreds of firemen, trimmers, greasers, and engineers maintained the ship's 159 furnaces, her 29 boilers (each having a diameter of 16 feet), and her three engines (one turbine and two reciprocating). Each cylinder of the reciprocating engines had a six-foot stroke.[7]

In keeping with Ismay's purpose, the *Titanic* offered luxurious first-class accommodations and unusually comfortable arrangements for second-class and third-class ("steerage") passengers. She had a gymnasium, a swimming pool, a Turkish bath, barber shops, libraries, a real restaurant and a real café (not just the customary dining saloons), and four 12-passenger elevators. Most of the amenities were intended for first- or second-class passengers—the wealthy cosmopolitans, on the one hand, and the thrifty, sober, small-town folk, on the other. ("You don't meet anyone rough [in] second class," one passenger assured his wife.[8]) Third-class accommodations, occupied mainly by hopeful emigrants, were plain and straightforwardly efficient, graceless but far from unhealthy or humiliating. Passengers in third class might well believe that their quarters were "as fine as first class had been twenty years earlier."[9]

A big selling point was *Titanic*'s promise of strength and dependability. She towered over her dock "like the side of a cliff"; yet she was, as the poet Thomas Hardy saw her, a "creature of cleaving wing."[10] The enormous power of the *Titanic*'s engines could drive her through any Atlantic storm. Her hull, which was divided into 16 watertight compartments, was designed to remain afloat if any two contiguous compartments were flooded. Because this was the worst accident her builders thought they needed to provide against, they regarded her as virtually unsinkable.

The *Titanic* appeared to be safe even from Britain's deepening political troubles. When transatlantic shipping was disrupted by a coal strike, White Star procured coal from other ships and gave it to *Titanic*. She began her maiden voyage from Southampton as scheduled, at noon on Wednesday, April 10, 1912. Bruce Ismay went along for the ride.

There was a bad moment, right at the start, when the liner *New York*, disturbed by *Titanic*'s passage through the harbor, broke her moorings and lunged toward the giant vessel. *Titanic* escaped, though narrowly. Passengers could choose to consider the incident either as a warning that every ship is vulnerable or as more evidence of *Titanic*'s power.[11] But the *Titanic* was soon on the open sea, bound for New York by way of Cherbourg, France, where she picked up wealthy travelers from Paris, and Queenstown (now Cobh), Ireland, where she picked up emigrants to the New World. By the time the ship left Queenstown on April 11, Ismay was accompanied by about 1,300 other passengers and 900 members of the crew.

What he did during the voyage was not remarkable enough for anyone to remember in detail.[12] He slept in his beautiful suite on B deck. He came to dinner with the other first-class passengers. He walked the decks, enjoying the unusually calm weather. When the ship stopped at Queenstown he conferred with the Chief Engineer about the possibility of trying her out at top speed on April 15 or 16—a trial that was never to take place. On Saturday afternoon, Mrs. Elisabeth Lines (as she would later report) overheard some talk between Ismay and Captain E.J. Smith in one of the *Titanic*'s public rooms. She would recall Ismay's expressing satisfaction in the *Titanic*'s speed and predicting that the ship would make New York harbor some time on Tuesday (rather than Wednesday morning as planned). This would not set any North Atlantic speed records, but it would beat the *Olympic*'s time on her own maiden voyage. Things were going so well that the *Titanic* might easily claim this little prize, if Ismay desired her to do so.[13]

Just before lunch on Sunday, April 14, Captain Smith found Ismay on A deck, talking with some other passengers. Smith silently handed him one of several wireless messages received that day, warning of ice near *Titanic*'s course. Ismay "glanced at" this curiosity and put it in his pocket. About 7:00 P.M. that evening, when the captain was walking out of the first-class smoking room, he saw Ismay sitting there and asked him to return the message. Ismay did so. The *Titanic* continued moving at 25 miles an hour—not her top speed, but a very respectable one—in the direction of the ice.

At 11:40 P.M., while Ismay was sleeping, an iceberg emerged from the moonless darkness directly in *Titanic*'s path. As the ship swerved to port, the little dark-blue mountain passed quietly along her starboard side, leaving beneath her waterline an intermittent series of small holes, breaks, and gashes, at least 250 feet long, and opening at least five watertight compartments to the sea. The *Titanic* began to sink.

Ismay's actions now become visible in brief, dramatic flashes. About 11:50, he appeared on the bridge, two decks above his cabin, wearing an overcoat hastily thrown over his pajamas. He asked Captain Smith if the *Titanic* was seriously damaged. Smith replied, "I am afraid she is." Ismay started to walk down into the vessel, but he encountered the Chief Engineer, who said that he thought the pumps would keep her afloat. Ismay returned to the bridge. There he overheard the captain saying something about lifeboats. The White Star line and its ship-builders had considered the *Titanic* so safe as to be "a lifeboat in herself." They had therefore not provided enough lifeboats for all the people on board. Ismay knew this.

The Managing Director next materialized on the port side of the boat deck. Crewmen had begun to uncover the lifeboats, but no passengers were waiting to use them. Ismay stood alone and silent. At perhaps 12:35 A.M., Third Officer Herbert Pitman was readying a lifeboat on the starboard side when he found himself standing next to a man "that was dressed in a dressing gown, with slippers on." The man said to him "very quietly, 'There is no time to waste.'" The man was J. Bruce Ismay.

Not recognizing him, and convinced that the ship was in no danger, Pitman proceeded with his work "in the usual [pre-sumably methodical] way." But the mysterious stranger insisted that the lifeboat should immediately be loaded with women and children. Pitman told him sharply that he was awaiting the captain's orders. "Very well," said Ismay. Pitman was now unsettled enough to walk to the bridge and ask the captain. Smith told him to "go ahead." With Ismay's assistance, Pitman loaded passengers into lifeboat No. 5. Ismay called out twice, "Are there any more women before this boat goes?", and a last woman shyly approached. "I am only a stewardess," she said. "Never mind," Ismay retorted. "You are a woman, take your place."

At some moment earlier in the night, Colonel Archibald Gracie, a first-class passenger, "saw Mr. Ismay with one of the officers" as they were "hurrying up the stairway." To Gracie, Ismay "looked very self contained, as though he was not fearful of anything, and that gave encouragement to my thought that perhaps the disaster was not anything particularly serious." But Gracie had an alternative memory of his impression. He remembered thinking that Ismay "was putting on as brave a face as possible so as to cause no alarm among the passengers." [14]

By the time No. 5 began its descent to the water, the crisis was plainly beginning to tell on Ismay. He hung on the davit from which No. 5 was suspended, and he shouted excitedly, "Lower away! Lower away! Lower away! Lower away!" It was too much for Fifth Officer Harold Lowe, who was down on the deck, trying to work the ropes. Lowe shouted at Ismay, "If you will get to hell out of that I shall be able to do something." Ismay did not reply. "Do you want me to lower away quickly?" Lowe demanded. "You will have me drown the whole lot of them."

Ismay walked silently away, and Lowe went on lowering No. 5. Once it was safely in the water, he turned to the next boat in line, No. 3. At that moment, there was an explosion and a burst of light; the *Titanic* was firing rockets. It was a moment of revelation. "Anybody knows," a passenger would write, "what rockets at sea mean. . . . Every one knew without being told that we were calling for help from any one who was near enough to see."[15] In the sudden brightness, Lowe saw Ismay standing quietly beside him, prepared to help with another boat.

By 1:40, a last lifeboat remained in the davits on the starboard side; Ismay thought it was the last one left on the ship. It was a boat with a wooden bottom and canvas sides—"collapsible" lifeboat C. It could carry 47 people. Ismay helped load the boat with about 30 women and children. All, or almost all, were third-class passengers. Hiding somewhere in the shadows at the bottom of the boat were four men later described as Chinese or Filipino "stowaways." Six crewmen also entered the lifeboat.[16]

An officer called out for more women. No one responded. Ismay looked around. His view to port was blocked by deck houses, but he could see the forward part of the starboard deck. No other passengers were visible. The sea was climbing up *Titanic*'s bow. The lifeboat was starting to move. This was the moment. Ismay climbed in. A certain Mr. William E. ("Billy") Carter, a sportsman from Bryn Mawr, Pennsylvania, appeared and climbed in too.

During the next five minutes, Collapsible C traveled with difficulty down the side of the *Titanic*, now listing sadly to port.[17]

7. The rescue ship *Carpathia*, a 13,500-ton steamer rated at 14 knots. Racing to *Titanic's* aid, she made it up to 17. *Courtesy of the Mariners' Museum, Newport News, Virginia.*

Thirty-five minutes after the boat reached the water and rowed away, Ismay could have seen the *Titanic* plunge beneath the ocean. But Ismay did not see it. He did not want to see it. He was rowing with his back to the ship. Afterwards, he was glad that he had done so.

Just before dawn, the Cunard liner *Carpathia* arrived at the scene. She had picked up *Titanic's* wireless distress call and had raced toward her position through a sea filled with icebergs. The *Carpathia's* decks were lined with lookouts, her lifeboats were swung out, her sides were hung with electric lights, her gangways were open, and she was firing rockets. Ismay climbed aboard the *Carpathia* at 6:15 A.M. He was safe.

"Black Against the Stars"

Testimony of Emily Borie Ryerson

At the time of collision I was awake and heard the engines stop, but felt no jar. My husband was asleep, so I rang and asked the steward, Bishop, what was the matter. He said, "There is talk of an iceberg, ma'am, and they have stopped, not to run into it."

I told him to keep me informed if there were any orders. It was bitterly cold, so I put on a warm wrapper and looked out the window (we were in the large cabins on the B deck, very far aft) and saw the stars shining and a calm sea, but heard no noise. It was 12 o'clock.

After about 10 minutes I went out in the corridor, and saw far off people hurrying on deck. A passenger ran by and called out, "Put on your life belts and come up on the boat deck." I said, "Where did you get those orders?" He said, "From the captain." I went back then and told Miss Bowen and my daughter, who were in the next room, to dress immediately, roused my husband and the two younger children, who were in a room on the other side, and then remembered my maid, who had a room near us. Her door was locked and I had some difficulty in waking her. By this time my husband was fully dressed, and we could hear the noise of feet tramping on the deck overhead.

He was quite calm and cheerful and helped me put the life belts on the children and on my maid. I was paralyzed with fear of not all getting on deck together in time, as there were seven of us. I would not let my younger daughter dress, but she only put on a fur coat, as I did over her nightgown. My husband cautioned us all to keep together, and we went up to A deck, where we found quite a group of people we knew. Everyone had on a life belt, and they all were very quiet and self-possessed.

We stood about there for quite a long time—fully half an hour, I should say. I know my maid ran down to the cabin and got some of my clothes. Then we were ordered to the boat deck. I only remember the second steward at the head of the stairs, who told us where to go. My chief thought and that of everyone else was, I know, not to make a fuss and to do as we were told. My husband joked with some of the women he knew, and I heard him say, "Don't you hear the band playing?"

I begged him to let me stay with him, but he said, "You must obey orders. When they say, 'Women and children to the boats' you must go when your turn comes. I'll stay with John Thayer. We will be all right. You take a boat going to New York." This referred to the belief that there was a circle of ships around waiting. The *Olympic*, the *Baltic*, were some of the names I heard. All this time we could hear the rockets going up—signals of distress.

Again, we were ordered down to A deck, which was partly inclosed. We saw people getting into boats, but waited our turn. There was a rough sort of steps constructed to get up to the window. My boy, Jack, was with me. An officer at the window said, "That boy can't go." My husband stepped forward and said, "Of course, that boy goes with his mother; he is only 13." So they let him pass. They also said, "No more boys."

I turned and kissed my husband, and as we left he and the other men I knew—Mr. Thayer, Mr. Widener, and others—were all standing there together very quietly. [Mrs. Ryerson's husband did not survive.] The decks were lighted, and as you went through the window it was as if you stepped out into the dark.

We were flung into the boats. There were two men—an officer inside and a sailor outside—to help us. I fell on top of the women who were already in the boat, and scrambled to the bow with my eldest daughter. Miss Bowen and my boy were in the stern and my second daughter was in the middle of the boat with my maid. Mrs. Thayer, Mrs. Widener, Mrs. Astor, and Miss Eustis were the only others I knew in our boat [No. 4].

Presently an officer called out from the upper deck, "How many women are there in that boat?" Someone answered, "Twenty-four." "That's enough; lower away."

The ropes seemed to stick at one end and the boat tipped, some one called for a knife, but it was not needed until we got into the water, as it was but a short distance, and I then realized for the first time how far the ship had sunk. The deck we left was only about 20 feet from the sea. I could see all the port-holes open and water washing in, and the decks still lighted.

Then they called out, "How many seamen have you," and they answered one. "That is not enough," said the officer, "I will send you another," and he sent a sailor down the rope. In a few minutes after several other men not sailors came down the ropes over the davits and dropped into our boat.

The order was given to pull away, then they rowed off—the sailors, the women, anyone—but made little progress; there was a confusion of orders; we rowed toward the stern, some one shouted something about a gangway [from which more passengers might be loaded], and no one seemed to know what to do. Barrels and chairs were being thrown overboard. Then suddenly, when we still seemed very near, we saw the ship was sinking rapidly.

I was in the bow of the boat with my daughter and turned to see the great ship take a plunge toward the bow, the two for-ward funnels seemed to lean and then she seemed to break in half as if cut with a knife, and as the bow went under the lights went out; the stern stood up for several minutes, black against the stars, and then that, too, plunged down, and there was no sound for what seemed like hours, and then began the cries for help of people drowning all around us, which seemed to go on forever.

Some one called out, "Pull for your lives, or you'll be sucked under," and everyone that could rowed like mad, I could see my younger daughter and Mrs. Thayer and Mrs. Astor rowing, but there seemed to be no suction. Then we turned to pick up some of those in the water. Some of the women protested, but others persisted, and we dragged in six or seven men; the men we rescued were principally stokers, stewards, sailors, etc., and were so chilled and frozen already they could hardly move. Two of them died in the stern later and many were raving and moaning and delirious most of the time.

We had no lights or compass. There were several babies in the boat, but there was no milk or water. (I believe these were all stowed away somewhere, but no one knew where, and as the bottom of the boat was full of water and the boat full of peo-ple it was very difficult to find anything.)

After the *Titanic* sank we saw no lights, and no one seemed to know what direction to take. Lowe, the officer in charge of the boat, had called out earlier for all to tie together, so we now heard his whistle, and as soon as we could make out the other boats in the dark, five of us were tied together, and we drifted about without rowing, as the sea was calm, waiting for the dawn.

It was very cold, and soon a breeze sprang up, and it was hard to keep our heavy boat bow on; but as the cries died down we could see dimly what seemed to be a raft with about 20 men standing on it, back to back. It was the overturned boat [Collapsible B, overturned as it was washed from the deck during *Titanic*'s last moments]; and as the sailors on our boat said we could still carry 8 or 10 more people, we called for another boat to volunteer and go to rescue them. So we two cut loose our painters and between us got all the men off. They were nearly gone and could not have held out much longer.

Then, when the sun rose we saw the *Carpathia* standing up about 5 miles away, and for the first time saw the icebergs all around us. The *Carpathia* steamed toward us until it was full daylight; then she stopped and began picking up boats.

American Inquiry, 1102–1104

CHAPTER 2

"He Ought to Have Gone Down with the Ship"

But Ismay's troubles had barely begun. He soon learned that two-thirds of the *Titanic's* passengers and crew (more than 1,500 people) had perished. They included the *Titanic's* captain, one of her designers, most of her crew, most of her second- and third-class passengers (losses among males in second class were over 90 percent), and most of the male passengers in first class—among them, such prominent people as John Jacob Astor and Benjamin Guggenheim. The lost also included Bruce Ismay's butler, Richard Fry, and his secretary, W.H. Harrison, whose presence on the ship had apparently slipped their employer's mind. Ismay was especially horrified to learn that many women had died. In a state of nervous collapse, he repaired to the cabin of the *Carpathia's* doctor and refused to leave. The doctor provided opiates. Ismay "kept repeating that he ought to have gone down with the ship." [18]

Many people agreed. In New York, where the *Carpathia* was heading, the newspapers were intensely interested in the question of why, as *The Wall Street Journal* put it, "the greatest or least official of the line" should have been saved while passengers were lost. Soon the papers would be calling Ismay "The Most-Talked-of Man in the World"—a dubious honor, especially when the title appeared in conjunction with such ominous terms as "public opinion," "on trial," and "pariah." [19]

The intellectuals were also starting to work themselves up. Some found it easy to decide the moral issues. Rear Admiral A.T. Mahan, the distinguished historian and theorist of naval power, wrote to the popular press to excoriate Ismay for failing to accept the duty of evacuating everyone else before saving himself. According to Mahan, to condone Ismay would be to undermine the essential principle of "individual responsibility." Brooks Adams—historian, descendant of presidents, and distinguished meddler with many theories—pronounced Ismay morally "responsible" for everything that had gone wrong with the *Titanic*. Adams said he could recall "nothing at once so cowardly and so brutal in recent history" as Ismay's escape in Collapsible C. Ismay should at least have "prove[d] his honesty and his sincerity by giving his life." Adams hoped Congress would "make it plain that such men cannot be kept in control of passenger ships if we can help it."[20]

The politicians were already in motion. An investigative committee of the United States Senate, hastily organized by William Alden Smith (Republican, Michigan), was determined to grab Ismay before he could get back to England. When the *Carpathia* reached New York on April 18, Senator Smith marched onto the ship, ignoring the "Please Do Not Knock" sign on Ismay's quarters, and summoned him to attend a hearing scheduled to open the very next morning in the East Room of the Waldorf-Astoria.[21]

If Bruce Ismay typified the business elite of the early twentieth century, William Alden Smith typified the populist political power. Having started out in life as a popcorn seller on the streets of Grand Rapids, Smith had become a wealthy lawyer, a newspaper owner, and a crusader against the House of Morgan and other big-business interests. He was an ingenuous busybody, cherishing the typically twentieth-century American assumption that if anything goes wrong, the United States government ought to do something about it.

Smith reacted to the sinking of the *Titanic* by calling the White House, only to discover that President Taft's conception of duty was not entirely up to date. The president was mourn-

8. Bruce Ismay (far right), painfully alone among his corporate associates, arrives in Washington for the post-*Titanic* inquiry. The special subcommittee of the Senate Committee on Commerce began hearing testimony in the Waldorf-Astoria in New York but soon moved its transactions to the seat of power. Ismay reluctantly followed, and was kept in Washington until the chairman of the committee was pleased to release him. He did not return to England until May 11, when he arrived on White Star's liner *Adriatic,* four weeks after the *Titanic*'s uncompleted voyage. *Stock Montage, Inc.*

ing the loss of his confidant, Major Archie Butt, a victim of the disaster, but he planned no immediate government action. The *Titanic*, after all, had been a vessel of British registry and had never managed to enter American waters.

So Smith decided that Congress should become involved, in the person of himself. His intention, as it matured, was to enable passengers or their survivors to sue White Star under the provisions of the Harter Act, which was helpful to plaintiffs who could show that officials of a steamship company had been aware of negligence, even though they had not caused it.[22]

Ismay began his testimony before Smith, his natural enemy, in the worst possible way. His description of his own conduct went as follows:

I was in bed myself, asleep, when the accident happened.
The ship sank, I am told, at 2.20.
That, sir, I think is all I can tell you.[23]

This could not have satisfied anyone's curiosity, let alone
Senator Smith's. To the delight of future historians but the
severe discomfiture of Ismay, Smith demanded information on
every conceivable point of contact between the disaster and the
Managing Director, including his possible influence on, and
therefore responsibility for, the ship's navigation; his conduct on
the boat deck; his conduct on the rescue ship; and his frustrated
desire to return to England. Smith called a long series of crewmen and passengers to testify about their experiences, with particular attention, whenever possible, to the conduct of Mr.
Ismay.

What emerged from this testimony was evidence that Ismay
had exerted very little influence on anything. For better or
worse, he had not told the captain what to do about icebergs.
He had not incited him to reach New York as fast as possible; he
had specifically not wanted that to happen. He had not
attempted to direct the launching of lifeboats, though he had
tried to help where he could. He had not deprived any other
passenger of a means of escape. He had not directed actions
aboard the rescue ship. He had not tried to direct a coverup. As
to the number of lifeboat accommodations, his ship had met,
and even exceeded, the regulations of the British Board of
Trade.

But should Ismay have gotten into a lifeboat?

Out in the provinces, where towns named "Ismay" were
considering a change,[24] the moral issue may have seemed that
starkly personal. But to Senator Smith, the real issue remained
that of corporate guilt—in many possible forms. He demanded
evidence that White Star officials had not tried to fool the public into believing that the *Titanic* had survived, so that they
could try to reinsure her. He demanded stockholders' records
from the Morgan holding company. He demanded that Dow,
Jones furnish complete information on the (minor) fluctua-

9. Loaded for bear: Senator William Alden Smith, chairman of the American investigative committee, strides toward the *Titanic* hearings. *Stock Montage, Inc.*

tions of the company's stock subsequent to the disaster. He demanded to know how Dow, Jones handled the news.

Smith even pursued the Marconi Company, whose wireless operators had summoned the *Carpathia* to save the *Titanic*'s surviving passengers. He subjected company officials, among them the great Guglielmo Marconi himself, to tireless and almost incredibly hostile questioning. He wanted to know whether they had connived with Ismay or White Star to block the news of *Titanic*'s fate. He also attempted to arouse public indignation about the help that Marconi officials had given *Carpathia*'s operator, and the surviving *Titanic* operator, to sell their personal reminiscences to the *New York Times*.

10. The American inquiry: Senator Smith faces us at the center of the table, writing something; Ismay (far right) ponders something. *Stock Montage, Inc.*

Smith's moral concerns seem to have been exacerbated by envy of Marconi's reputation: "As [Smith] later confided to friends, he could never resist swinging at 'handmade halos.'"[25] It did no good for Marconi and his fellow executives to show, over and over again, that they had received no profit from the transaction with the *New York Times,* that they had facilitated it because they believed that their heroic employees deserved a chance to make some extra money, and that the arrangement, which was suggested to the operators when they were entering New York harbor and which resulted in the immediate publication of their stories, had not exactly delayed the nation's news. Marconi reminded Smith that people had the right to sell their stories. But Smith cudgeled him into agreeing that the practice should be discouraged, and he made him repeat, like a schoolchild, a declaration that he was testifying before Smith "voluntarily." Then Smith bullied Marconi's subordinates about their "vicious" practice.[26]

Bullying tactics were also applied to Ismay. Rejecting his vigorous requests that he be allowed to return to England, Smith angrily insisted on reserving him for future testimony. Smith then tried to get him to confess that he had been accorded complete fairness and courtesy. During smoking breaks in the hallways, Ismay had entertained reporters with angry remarks about Senator Smith's procedures and with outbreaks of revived confidence in his own innocence. But he publicly acquiesced, testifying that he had met with no "discourtesy" and had "no fault to find."[27]

Smith had used the political power to humble Ismay and (in the vernacular expression) make Ismay like it. He had done something more important. In the words of a friendly commentator, he had "bent an instrument [the congressional hearing], constitutionally intended for the sole purpose of obtaining data useful to legislation," into a means of "mobilizing the power of public opinion" about social and moral issues.[28] One should not exaggerate Smith's inventiveness; he was part of a trend. But he provided a precedent for all those far-reaching inquisitions to which subsequent generations have become

11. The American inquiry: Ismay, testifying, tries to thrust matters into the proper light. *UPI/Corbis-Bettmann.*

neither "wise" nor necessary, they had to be carried out in order "to satisfy the public, on whom we are dependent for our living."[30]

However that may have been, Senator Smith escaped from his hearings with the legislative proposals that he desired, and Ismay escaped for the second time from the *Titanic.* He took ship for England, leaving the great liner sinking behind him in a sea of regulatory proposals.

"Then They Did Not See Me"

Testimony of Daniel Buckley, Irish Immigrant, 21 Years of Age

Senator Smith: How did you happen to come over to America?

Mr. Buckley: I wanted to come over here to make some money. I came in the *Titanic* because she was a new steamer.

The night of the wreck I was sleeping in my room on the *Titanic*, in the steerage. There were three other boys from the same place sleeping in the same room with me.

I heard some terrible noise and I jumped out on the floor, and the first thing I knew my feet were getting wet; the water was just coming in slightly. I told the other fellows to get up, that there was something wrong and that the water was coming in. They only laughed at me. One of them says: "Get back into bed. You are not in Ireland now."

I got on my clothes as quick as I could, and the three other fellows got out. The room was very small, so I got out, to give them room to dress themselves.

Two sailors came along, and they were shouting: "All up on deck! unless you want to get drowned."

When I heard this, I went for the deck as quick as I could. . . .

Senator Smith: What became of those other three boys?

Mr. Buckley: I can not say. I did not see them any more after leaving the room where I parted from them.

Senator Smith: They were lost?

Mr. Buckley: Yes; they were lost.

Senator Smith: Was there any effort made on the part of the officers or crew to hold the steerage passengers in the steerage?

Mr. Buckley: I do not think so.

Senator Smith: Were you permitted to go on up to the top deck without any interference?

Mr. Buckley: Yes, sir. They tried to keep us down at first on our steerage deck. They did not want us to go up to the first-class place at all.

Senator Smith: Who tried to do that?

Mr. Buckley: I can not say who they were. I think they were sailors.

Senator Smith: What happened then? Did the steerage passengers try to get out?

Mr. Buckley: Yes; they did. There was one steerage passenger there, and he was getting up the steps, and just as he was going in a little gate a fellow came along and chucked him down; threw him down into the steerage place. This fellow got excited, and he ran after him, and he could not find him. He got up over the little gate. He did not find him.

Senator Smith: What gate do you mean?

Mr. Buckley: A little gate just at the top of the stairs going into the first-class deck. . . . The first-class deck was higher up than the steerage deck, and there were some steps leading up to it; 9 or 10 steps, and a gate just at the top of the steps.

Senator Smith: Was the gate locked?

Mr. Buckley: It was not locked at the time we made the attempt to get up there, but the sailor, or whoever he was, locked it. So that this fellow that went up after him broke the lock on it, and he went after the fellow that threw him down. He said if he could get hold of him he would throw him into the ocean.

Senator Smith: Did these passengers in the steerage have any opportunity at all of getting out?

Mr. Buckley: Yes; they had.

Senator Smith: What opportunity did they have?

Mr. Buckley: I think they had as much chance as the first and second class passengers.

Senator Smith: After this gate was broken?

Mr. Buckley: Yes; because they were all mixed. All the steerage passengers went up on the first-class deck at this time, when the gate was broken. They all got up there. They could not keep them down. . . .

When I got up on the deck I saw everyone having those life belts on only myself; so I got sorry, and said I would go back again where I was sleeping and get one of those life preservers; because there was one there for each person.

I went back again, and just as I was going down the last flight of stairs the water was up four steps, and dashing up. I did not go back into the room, because I could not. When I went back toward the room the water was coming up three steps up the stairs, or four steps; so I did not go any farther. I got back on the deck again, and just as I got back there, I was looking around to see if I could get any of those life belts, and I met a first-class passenger, and he had two. He gave me one, and fixed it on me.

Then the lifeboats were preparing. There were five lifeboats sent out. I was in the sixth. I was holding the ropes all the time, helping to let down the five lifeboats that went down first, as well as I could.

When the sixth lifeboat was prepared, there was a big crowd of men standing on the deck. And they all jumped in. So I said I would take my chance with them.

Senator Smith: Who were they?

Mr. Buckley: Passengers and sailors and firemen, mixed. There were no ladies there at the same time.

When they jumped, I said I would go too. I went into the boat. Then two officers came along and said all of the men could come out. And they brought a lot of steerage passengers with them; and they were mixed, every way, ladies and gentlemen. And they said all the men could get out and let the ladies in. But six men were left in the boat. I think they were firemen and sailors.

I was crying. There was a woman in the boat, and she had thrown her shawl over me, and she told me to stay in there. I believe she was Mrs. Astor. [She was not; she was a woman whose name we do not know.] Then they did not see me, and the boat was lowered down into the water, and we rowed away out from the steamer.

American Inquiry, 1018, 1019–1020, 1018

CHAPTER 3

"Exercise Your Own Common Sense"

Although Ismay had extricated himself from America, he was not yet free. On reaching home, he was summoned to appear before another body of investigators, a court convened by the British Board of Trade.

The *Titanic* story was now in the hands of Lord Mersey, a canny old jurist who looked like the little man in the Monopoly game. Mersey presided over the court as Wreck Commissioner, assisted by Attorney-General Sir Rufus Isaacs and attorneys representing White Star, the third-class passengers, labor unions, and various other interests. The record of the 36-day British inquiry is a monument of intelligence and well-grounded diversity of judgment. Mersey and the lawyers practicing before him showed distinguished analytical ability, whether they maintained, with Attorney-General Isaacs, that the *Titanic* was lost through "negligent navigation," or they insisted, with Sir Robert Finlay, counsel for White Star, that she was lost to "circumstances which are quite unprecedented, and could not have been anticipated."[31]

Lord Mersey took nearly an opposite approach from that of Senator Smith. Smith began with moral outrage and ended with proposals for government regulation; Mersey emphasized problems of regulation while trying—without success—to avoid

12. Ismay (far right), Mrs. Ismay, and Ismay's business associate Harold Sanderson hurry through London toward the British inquiry. *Corbis-Bettmann*.

issues of moral culpability, which he considered beyond the competence of his court. Personal morality kept slipping *away* from Smith's inquiry; it kept slipping *into* Mersey's.

Mersey was skeptical, as Smith was not, about the usefulness of regulation. He even entertained a thought that the twentieth century would come to regard as virtually heretical, the idea that consumers might bear some responsibility for their own safety. Reflecting on evidence that ships customarily proceeded at full speed despite the danger of ice, Mersey asked, "Have you ever considered who the people are who are really responsible for it, if it is a wrong custom or practice? Is it not the passengers?"[32] Passengers wanted speed; captains and corporations obliged.

And there was only so much that could be done with consumers, even consumers like Mersey himself. When one of the attending lawyers, W.D. Harbinson, suggested that regulations should require the posting of certain instructional notices to passengers, Mersey responded:

> Exercise your own common sense. Do you think, Mr. Harbinson, that if such notices were stuck up, any body would ever read them[?] Judging for myself I do not believe anyone would ever read them; I never should. Perhaps I ought to. The question is, What would happen, not what ought to happen. Have you ever been on board a ship?
>
> **Mr. Harbinson:** I have never been to America, but, if I may relate my personal experience, every time I go across the Channel one of the first things I do is to read the notices.
>
> **Mersey:** You are one of the most extraordinary men I have ever come across. The first thing I do, if it is about the middle of the day, when I get on a cross-Channel steamer is to get some lunch, and the notion that I should go about the decks or about the ship reading all the notices that are stuck up never occurred to me.[33]

Mersey was quite prepared to advocate new regulations, if he thought them useful. But his mind focused on risks. There was a risk to every form of travel—even walking.[34] Safety could not be guaranteed. Regulation also had its risks. It was a human choice; it might be unwise or even harmful. To Senator Smith, the "laxity" of current lifeboat regulations was an obvious reason for stricter regulations. To Lord Mersey, apparent "laxity" might represent an adjustment to risks that he didn't understand. Again, there were hard choices to be made. He was approaching a hazardous area, and he would proceed with caution.

Along the way, he amassed twice as much evidence as Senator Smith, although he was constantly trying to exclude irrelevant or unhelpful information. He was reluctant, for example, to summon passengers to testify, thinking that they would provide a less educated view of issues than the one that crew members and technical experts could develop. For Mersey and the Attorney-General, Bruce Ismay was not a high priority. They wanted to know how the *Titanic* was built, what happened in her engine room, how hard it was to reach her boat deck, what

13. Lord Mersey, the Wreck Commissioner, head of the British inquiry, with his son. An agile mind in an awkward body, Mersey tried to face some of the problems of the *Titanic,* and to outrun others. *Courtesy of the Mariners' Museum, Newport News, Virginia.*

risks were involved in launching her boats, what risks were run in the whole affair. Mersey did not know if regulations could reduce such risks; he meant to find out.

Nevertheless, he believed that neither risks nor rules could relieve responsible individuals of their duty to use good judgment, whoever the individuals were. When Ismay was finally examined, on days 16 and 17 of the British investigation, this was the issue. Was Ismay responsible, in some sense, for the decisions made on board the *Titanic*, and if so, did he use good judgment?

Mersey's inquiry considered evidence of a degree of involvement, which, though relatively slight, might imply responsibility. Hadn't Ismay suggested that a speed trial be held at some time before the ship reached New York? That was consultation, perhaps supervision. And hadn't the captain shown him the wireless warning that ice might be encountered at such and such a place? In response, Ismay claimed that he "had nothing to do with the navigation," that he intentionally kept away from it, and that he didn't even understand "latitude and longitude." [35] He demonstrated his innocence of navigation by a number of absurdly uninformed comments. If Ismay had been in charge of the *Titanic*, she would never have gotten as far as she had.

But what about the lifeboats? Do you remember discussing the number of lifeboats that the *Titanic* should carry? "No, I do not." When you got into Collapsible C, you saw no other passengers waiting to enter—but do you know whether there was an attempt to call more of them up to the boat deck? "That I do not know." Did you inquire? "No, I did not." Why didn't you yourself go to see whether there were more passengers for the lifeboats? "I presumed that there were people down below who were sending the people up." So you thought that everybody had already come up? "I knew," Ismay answered candidly, "that everybody could not be up." [36]

It was a bad moment. A worse one followed. Where do you think all those other people were? "I can only suppose the passengers had gone to the after end of the ship." You could not see them? "I presume they went there. I was really not thinking about it."[37]

It is true that Ismay could not possibly assess the situation at the after end of the ship from his position near the fore end of the giant boat deck. But he was really not thinking about it.

Suddenly, the issue had transformed itself from a problem of action into a problem of thought. It was hard enough to say whether Ismay had a responsibility to save everyone else before trying to save himself. Many people said that he had such a responsibility; no one had succeeded in demonstrating it. But it would be much harder to decide whether he had a responsibility to think through this issue of responsibility, to try the case within himself, weighing all the available evidence, while he was standing, at that moment, next to Collapsible C.

The question embarrassed Ismay. It embarrassed everyone. The problem was basic; the tools for handling it were hopelessly inadequate. Mersey put an end to Ismay's reminiscences and proceeded, with obvious relief, to aspects of the investigation more closely associated with possible regulatory reforms.

Much later, during final arguments, A. Clement Edwards, one of the labor lawyers, went after Ismay. He, Edwards claimed, had been no ordinary passenger on the *Titanic*, and he had had "special moral obligations" to the other passengers. Mersey replied, "I do not think I can deal with moral duties." This did not stop White Star's counsel from defending Ismay's decision as to the extent of his moral duty. He invited Mersey to analyze the risks that Ismay confronted on the boat deck. Ismay could have gone searching for other passengers to put into Collapsible C, but was there any chance that he could have brought them to the boat in time? No; and there was every chance that he would have sacrificed his own life in trying to do so. That wouldn't have been duty; that would have been "suicide."[38]

Mersey devoted one paragraph of his report to Ismay and the affair of Collapsible C. He rejected the argument that Ismay had a "moral duty . . . to wait on board until the vessel foundered. . . . Had he not jumped in he would merely have added one more life, namely, his own, to the number of those lost." [39] The report recommended that vessels slow down at night in the presence of ice. It recommended that vessels be required to carry lifeboats and liferafts for all, whenever practicable. It recommended various other regulatory reforms, and further study of still others.

Ismay had escaped again.

"Was It Your View that the Ship Was an Unsinkable Ship?"

Testimony of George Moore, Able Seaman

Mr. Moore: I went on the starboard side of the boat deck and helped clear the boats; swung three of the boats out; helped to lower No. 5 and No. 7. When we swung No. 3 out, I was told to jump in the boat and pass the ladies in. I was told that by the first officer. After we got so many ladies in, and there were no more about, we took in men passengers. We had 32 in the boat, all told, and then we lowered away. . . .

Senator Newlands: Why did you not take more than 32 in that boat?

Mr. Moore: That is not up to me, sir; that was for the officer on top.

Senator Newlands: Did you not think at the time that it ought to have been more heavily loaded?

Mr. Moore: It seemed pretty full, but I dare say we could have jammed more in. The passengers were not anxious to get in the boats; they were not anxious to get in the first lot of boats.

Senator Newlands: What was your feeling at the time?

Mr. Moore: I thought, myself, that there was nothing serious the matter until we got away from the ship and she started settling down.

Senator Newlands: You would have been as well pleased to have stayed on the ship as to get on the lifeboat?

Mr. Moore: I would at that time, sir.

Senator Newlands: How soon after getting in the water did you see that the ship was sinking?

Mr. Moore: After we pulled a distance away, sir, you could see her head gradually going down.

Senator Newlands: Where were the most of the passengers on the ship at the time you left the ship and when you could see the passengers?

Mr. Moore: When we started lowering the boats all I saw was first-class ladies and gentlemen all lined up with their life belts on and coming out of the saloon [probably the vestibule of the forward first-class staircase, which led to the boat deck]. I could not say what was on the after part of the ship at all. There was a lot of space between the boats.

Senator Newlands: Where were the steerage passengers, do you think?

Mr. Moore: I could not answer that. I should say that they were making for the boat deck as well.

Senator Newlands: There was nothing to prevent them from coming up to any part of the ship, was there?

Mr. Moore: No, sir.

Senator Newlands: Did they show any disorder?

Mr. Moore: No, sir.

Senator Newlands: Was it your view that the ship was an unsinkable ship?

Mr. Moore: That was the talk.

Senator Newlands: Was that the general idea of the crew on the ship?

Mr. Moore: Yes, sir.

Senator Newlands: You knew that there were not enough boats to accommodate the entire crew and the passenger list?

Mr. Moore: I knew there were only 20 boats, and I knew they would not carry all the people.

American Inquiry, 560–62

"I Remember the Ship Went Down"

Testimony of Frederick Barrett, Stoker, in Charge of Lifeboat No. 13

The Solicitor-General [Sir John Simon]: You have told us you saw some third-class passengers coming up to where these boats were, as far as you know. Had you got some of those third-class passengers in your boat?

Mr. Barrett: All the women were getting up in the boat at the last of it, and the women were there till there was no more. The men stood all in one line when I was getting up there. I saw them standing in one line, as if at attention waiting for an order to get into the boat, against the back of the [deck] house.

The Solicitor-General: Was there good order on deck?

Mr. Barrett: Yes.

The Solicitor-General: Did you see who was keeping them back, if anybody was?

Mr. Barrett: I did not.

The Solicitor-General: Was there any officer there?

Mr. Barrett: No.

The Solicitor-General: They were keeping good order without him?

Mr. Barrett: Yes.

The Solicitor-General: You say you had got about 70 people in your boat. Did you pick up anybody out of the sea or not?

Mr. Barrett: No.

The Solicitor-General: Had you any room to?

Mr. Barrett: No.

The Solicitor-General: There are two or three questions that we ask everybody about these boats; I will put them to you. As far as you know, was there any compass in the boat No. 13?

Mr. Barrett: I did not look.

The Solicitor-General: At any rate, no compass was used as far as you know?

Mr. Barrett: The only thing I looked for was a light.

The Solicitor-General: Was there any light in the boat?

Mr. Barrett: No.

The Solicitor-General: Was there any water?

Mr. Barrett: I did not look.

The Solicitor-General: Biscuits?

Mr. Barrett: I did not look.

The Solicitor-General: I gather, Barrett, really, that you felt the cold so much that you do not remember very much?

Mr. Barrett: No; I remember the ship went down.

The Solicitor-General: You remember the ship going down?

Mr. Barrett: Yes; then I must have fallen asleep.

The Solicitor-General: You said one of the women put a cloak over you?

Mr. Barrett: Yes.

British Inquiry, 69

"Well, Boys, Do Your Best"

After the conclusion of the British inquiry, the Managing Director of the White Star line began to fade from the popular consciousness. But an impression remained, and it was not very flattering. It was associated with a certain general impression of the *Titanic* herself. Scholars of the disaster have routinely recorded this impression, and perpetuated it. "The *Titanic*," one says,

> was the incarnation of man's arrogance in equating size with security; his pride in intellectual (apart from spiritual) mastery; his blindness to the consequences of wasteful extravagance; and his superstitious faith in materialism and technology.[40]

In many cases, the definition of "man" is significantly narrowed. It is used to mean capitalists or corporate executives like J. Bruce Ismay, while "blindness" is understood as a condition naturally allied to competition or the profit motive. Thus we hear about "the overweening attitude which led entrepreneurs to pursue amazing but erratic advances in technology at breakneck speed."[41] Gifted with enough technological arrogance, capitalists and the people who worked for them could happily blind themselves to the risks they took with lives and property—including, though this is seldom emphasized, their own lives and property.

14. *Titanic's* master, Captain Edward J. Smith, reputedly the best-paid captain on the North Atlantic. Smith always took a good picture, but his personality remains a blur. Here he seems vaguely troubled. Or does he? *Courtesy of the Mariners' Museum, Newport News, Virginia.*

So runs a message found in a bottle on the shore of the Hebrides, after the liner *Pacific* disappeared in 1856. On February 11, 1893, the White Star cargo ship *Naronic* sailed from Liverpool, bound for New York. On March 4, two lifeboats were sighted, 300 miles apart. They were empty. No one knows what happened; it could have been an iceberg.[45]

A fatal encounter with ice was a small risk, to be sure, but one not easy to calculate. What does one do in the face of such risks? One consults experience—one's own experience and the experience preserved in custom. A long parade of North Atlantic captains testified before Lord Mersey that when they sailed under *Titanic* conditions (iceberg warnings, darkness, but good weather, with clear visibility) they never slowed down, and neither did anybody else. They could still see no reason to slow down—no more reason than you see to slow down or stop as soon as the radio warns you that there is some debris on the highway, up ahead. You believe you can wait till the hazard appears. That is what they thought, too. So when Captain Smith maintained *Titanic*'s speed, despite ice warnings, he was not being mindlessly irresponsible; he was following the custom of his profession.

But the talk of weather introduces more hazards to deduction. The weather on April 14 was *exceptionally* good; there were *no* waves. Such conditions, Mersey was repeatedly told, might be seen only once in a lifetime. This good weather meant good sailing. It also meant that no surf would break at an iceberg's foot. Icebergs would therefore be doubly hard to see.

Captain Smith knew that. But he believed that an iceberg could still be seen if the night remained clear.[46] This sounds very foolish, until one reads the testimony of the British inquiry's old sea dogs. They maintained that the glow of a white iceberg would be visible even on the darkest night.

But what about a *black* iceberg? Ah, that might be a problem. But how often does one see such a thing? A very experienced captain told Lord Mersey that he never even heard of black icebergs before he read about them "in the papers." Perhaps, suggested the Attorney-General, people don't know how many black icebergs they encounter *without* being able to see them.[47] Unless, of course, they run into them.

Assume, however, that black icebergs are rare. A flat calm on the North Atlantic is also rare. The conjunction of a black iceberg, a flat calm, and a large, fast ship is an exceptionally rare, perhaps an unprecedented, circumstance. Now, what deduction

do you make from that? Do you agree with counsel for the
White Star line, who argued that unprecedented circumstances
cannot be guarded against? Or do you agree with the Attorney-
General, who argued that "unusual conditions necessitate
unusual precautions"? Well, said Lord Mersey, unusual conditions don't excuse you unless they are so unusual that you are
not even aware of them.[48]

Captain Smith's moral responsibility must bear some relationship to his awareness of risk, but no one has ever been able
to compute either the risk or the awareness. After 87 years of
Titanic books, and substantial biographical research, the captain
remains an enigmatic figure. There was something about him
that inspired passengers to trust him. Probably it was his professional manner, pleasant but self-contained. From this evidence,
passengers might have inferred one of two things: either that
Smith was thinking intently, or that he was not thinking at all.
They took the risk of inferring the former.

Nobody knows exactly what Smith thought about his own
risks on that strangely calm Atlantic night. Nobody knows what
he had in mind, earlier in the voyage, when he failed to exercise
such humdrum duties as holding lifeboat drill and developing
plans for managing emergencies. The cause of his neglect may
have been hubris, an arrogant faith in his vessel's safety. In light
of what I said above, it may have been a well-founded faith that
simply happened to be wrong. Some people believe it was an
old man's forgetfulness—yet Smith was only 62 years of age and
was not necessarily, as is usually reported, on the verge of retire-
ment. Whether he was ready to retire or not, both his reputation and his life were at stake in the protection of his ship and
passengers. Also at stake, apparently, was an annual bonus of
£1,000 that White Star promised for returning its ships "in
good order."[49]

Whatever one believes about Smith's possible hubris or forgetfulness, neither of them can explain what he did, and didn't
do, after he realized (very quickly) that the *Titanic* was sinking.
He failed to issue a general evacuation call, either because he
wanted to prevent panic—which is the usual explanation—or

15. The perfection of objects never meant for use: A row of the *Titanic*'s lifeboats. *Courtesy of the Mariners' Museum, Newport News, Virginia.*

because he could not make up his mind to issue one. He allowed officers to go off and prepare lifeboats, without telling them to follow up by actually using them; hence Ismay's confrontation with Third Officer Pitman on the boat deck, and the strangely idyllic atmosphere that some people found on the upper decks even after the crash. Perhaps Smith was afraid that he might cause panic if he rushed anybody into doing anything.

As the night went on, he became very intent on getting people into lifeboats, but he failed to give any clear organization to the effort or to mobilize his officers to act in concert. Many of the crew worked hard to get passengers up to the boat deck; a few decided to do the opposite and tried to keep third-class passengers from crossing into first- and second-class territory. Others had no idea of what to do. On deck, volunteers wandered from one boat station to another, helping out as best they could.

Meanwhile, Smith appeared and disappeared in various loca-
tions, giving brief orders to various individuals and involving
himself personally in a variety of tasks. He provided an example
of stoic calm. But none of this amounted to effective leadership,
which would have required distinct and comprehensive delega-
tion of authority. Reviewing Smith's mysterious failure to organize the evacuation, a historian of the disaster argues that

> the real enemies that night . . . were lack of time and poor leader-
> ship, not the shortage of lifeboats. Even if they had had the num-
> ber [of] lifeboats they needed, it is impossible to see how they
> could have launched them.[50]

Did Smith's final mistakes result from a failure to assume personal responsibility, or from an attempt to assume too much of
it? No one can say. None of the testimony that emerged from
the disaster sheds any light on this; testimony could not even
establish how he came to die. According to one witness,

> He said, "Well, boys, do your best for the women and children,
> and look out for yourselves." He walked on[to] the bridge.[51]

Soon after, the ship went down.

It is evident, however, that considerable loss of life resulted
directly from an excess of moral responsibility on the part of
people who were working to save lives. The captain, and everybody else, believed that the policy in regard to lifeboats should
be "women and children first." They thought that was the right
principle. But what exactly did it mean? On the starboard side
of the boat deck, where Bruce Ismay happened to be, it meant
"women and children first, then men." On the port side, the
interpretation was more puritanical; there it was "women and
children only": when all the women and children in the vicinity
had entered a lifeboat, it was lowered away, whether it was full
or not. Men who could have been saved were left to perish;
some of the men who enforced the rule proceeded to die by it.[52]
As one of Lord Mersey's assistants suggested, "women and children first" may also have produced the kind of delays that

allowed boats to be launched with unused spaces. Time had to be taken to separate women and children from associated males, and sometimes just to find enough women. Then, since time kept growing shorter, there was pressure to launch the boats, even if they were not full.[53]

An excess of moral responsibility also led officers to worry about lowering boats that were filled to capacity, for fear they would buckle and dump their passengers into the sea. The boats were perfectly sound, but the *Titanic*'s officers did not know that, or trust their knowledge. They wanted to save people, not to kill them; as a result, they killed many people who would have fitted safely into the boats but who were not invited to enter. Moral principles helped to create a situation in which boat accommodations meant for 1,178 people were used by only about 700. Like most other things connected with the *Titanic*, morality presented a dark and dangerous surface as well as a brave and bright one.

We have now moved very far from the conception of the *Titanic* that lingers in the popular imagination, that of a ship whose passengers were doomed by technological arrogance and corporate greed. That *Titanic* belongs to the world of myth. The *Titanic* of fact, the *Titanic* on which we are now sailing (or sinking), was imperilled by obstacles much more difficult to chart—the incalculability of certain risks, the opaqueness of certain intentions, the unpredictability of results from even the best intentions, and the reversibility of "obvious" deductions from "known" facts.

"We Ain't Got Much Show, Anyhow"

Testimony of Olaus Abelseth

Senator Smith: How old are you?

Mr. Abelseth: Twenty-six years of age in June.

Senator Smith: Did you sail on the *Titanic?*

Mr. Abelseth: Yes.

Senator Smith: From what port?

Mr. Abelseth: From Southampton.

Senator Smith: Where had you been?

Mr. Abelseth: I had been in Norway. I left here last fall.

Senator Smith: Where do you live now?

Mr. Abelseth: My home is in South Dakota, where I have my homestead.

Senator Smith: I wish you would tell the reporter when you first knew of this collision, and what you did, and where you were in the ship. I believe you were a steerage passenger?

Mr. Abelseth: Yes, sir.

Senator Smith: In the forward part of the ship?

Mr. Abelseth: Yes. I was in compartment [deck] G on the ship.

Senator Smith: Go ahead and tell us what happened.

Mr. Abelseth: I went to bed about 10 o'clock Sunday night, and I think it was about 15 minutes to 12 when I woke up; and there was another man in the same room—two of us in the same room—and he said to me, "What is that?" I said, "I don't know, but we had better get up." So we did get up and put our clothes on, and we two went up on deck in the forward part of the ship.

Then there was quite a lot of ice on the starboard part of the ship. They wanted us to go down again, and I saw one of the officers, and I said to him: "Is there any danger?" He said,

"No." I was not satisfied with that, however, so I went down and told my brother-in-law and my cousin, who were in the same compartment there. They were not in the same room, but they were just a little ways from where I was. I told them about what was happening, and I said they had better get up. Both of them got up and dressed, and we took our overcoats and put them on. We did not take any life belts with us. There was no water on the deck at that time.

We walked to the hind part of the ship and got two Norwegian girls up. One was in my charge and one was in charge of the man who was in the same room with me. He was from the same town that I came from. The other one was just 16 years old, and her father told me to take care of her until we got to Minneapolis. The two girls were in a room in the hind part of the ship, in the steerage.

We all went up on deck and stayed there. We walked over to the port side of the ship, and there were five of us standing, looking, and we thought we saw a light.

Senator Smith: On what deck were you standing?

Mr. Abelseth: Not on the top deck, but on—I do not know what you call it, but it is the hind part, where the sitting room is; and then there is a kind of a little space in between, where they go up on deck. It was up on the boat deck [really the after well deck, deck C], the place for the steerage passengers on the deck. We were then on the port side there, and we looked out at this light. I said to my brother-in-law: "I can see it plain, now. It must be a light."

Senator Smith: How far away was it?

Mr. Abelseth: I could not say, but it did not seem to be so very far. I thought I could see this mast light, the front mast light. That is what I thought I could see [a light from the *Californian*?; see pp. 76–79, 95, below].

A little while later there was one of the officers who came and said to be quiet, that there was a ship coming. That is all he said. He did not say what time, or anything. That is all he said.

So I said to them, we had better go and get the life belts, as we had not brought them with us. So my cousin and I went down to get the life belts for all of us. When we came up again we carried the life belts on our arms for a while.

There were a lot of steerage people there that were getting on one of these cranes that they had on deck, that they used to lift things with. They can lift about two and a half tons, I believe. These steerage passengers were crawling along on this, over the railing, and away up to the boat deck. A lot of them were doing that.

Senator Smith: They could not get up there in any other way?

Mr. Abelseth: The gate was shut.

Senator Smith: Was it locked?

Mr. Abelseth: I do not know whether it was locked, but it was shut so that they could not go that way.

A while later these girls were standing there, and one of the officers came and hollered for all of the ladies to come up on the boat deck. The gate was opened and these two girls went up.

We stayed a little while longer, and then they said, "Everybody." I do not know who that was, but I think it was some of the officers that said it. I could not say that, but it was somebody that said "everybody." We went up. We went over to the port side of the ship, and there were just one or two boats on the port side that were lost [were left]. Anyway, there was one. We were standing there looking at them lowering this boat. We could see them, some of the crew helping take the ladies in their arms and throwing them into the lifeboats. We saw them lower this boat, and there were no more boats on the port side.

So we walked over to the starboard side of the ship, and just as we were standing there, one of the officers came up and he said just as he walked by, "Are there any sailors here?"

I did not say anything. I have been a fishing man for six years, and, of course, this officer walked right by me and asked: "Are there any sailors here?" I would have gone, but my brother-in-law and my cousin said, in the Norwegian language, as we were speaking Norwegian: "Let us stay here together." I do not know, but I think the officer wanted some help to get some of these collapsible boats out. All he said was: "Are there any sailors here?" I did not say anything, but I have been used to the ocean for a long time. I commenced to work on the ocean when I was 10 years old with my dad fishing. I kept that up until I came to this country.

Then we stayed there, and we were just standing still there. We did not talk very much. Just a little ways from us I saw there was an old couple standing there on the deck, and I heard this man say to the lady, "Go into the lifeboat and get saved." He put his hand on her shoulder and I think he said: "Please get into the lifeboat and get saved." She replied: "No; let me stay with you." I could not say who it was, but I saw that he was an old man. I did not pay much attention to him, because I did not know him.

I was standing there, and I asked my brother-in-law if he could swim and he said no. I asked my cousin if he could swim and he said no. So we could see the water coming up, the bow of the ship was going down, and there was a kind of an explosion. We could hear the popping and cracking, and the deck raised up and got so steep that the people could not stand on their feet on the deck. So they fell down and slid on the deck into the water right on the ship. Then we hung onto a rope in one of the davits. We were pretty far back at the top deck.

My brother-in-law said to me, "We had better jump off or the suction will take us down." I said, "No. We won't jump yet. We ain't got much show anyhow, so we might as well stay as long as we can." So he stated again, "We must jump off." But I said, "No; not yet." So, then, it was only about 5 feet down to the water when we jumped off. It was not much of a jump. Before that we could see the people were jumping over. There was water coming onto the deck, and they were jumping over, then, out in the water.

My brother-in-law took my hand just as we jumped off, and my cousin jumped at the same time. When we came into the water, I think it was from the suction—or anyway we went under, and I swallowed some water. I got a rope tangled around me, and I let loose of my brother-in-law's hand to get away from the rope. I thought then, "I am a goner." That is what I thought when I got tangled up in this rope. But I came on top again, and I was trying to swim, and there was a man—lots of them were floating around—and he got me on the neck like that [illustrating] and pressed me under, trying to get on top of me. I said to him, "Let go." Of course, he did not pay any attention to that, but I got away from him. Then there was another man, and he hung on to me for a while, but he let go.

Then I swam; I could not say, but it must have been about 15 or 20 minutes. It could not have been over that. Then I saw something dark ahead of me. I did not know what it was, but I swam toward that, and it was one of those collapsible boats.

When we jumped off of the ship, we had life preservers on. There was no suction from the ship at all. I was lying still, and I thought "I will try to see if I can float on the life belt without help from swimming," and I floated easily on the life belt.

When I got on this raft or collapsible boat [Collapsible A, which had been washed off the ship before its canvas sides could be raised, and remained full of water], they did not try to push me off, and they did not do anything for me to get on. All they said when I got on there was, "Don't capsize the boat." So I hung onto the raft for a little while before I got on.

Some of them were trying to get up on their feet. They were sitting down or lying down on the raft. Some of them fell into the water again. Some of them were frozen; and there were two dead, that they threw overboard.

I got on this raft or collapsible boat and raised up, and then I was continually moving my arms and swinging them around to keep warm. There was one lady aboard this raft, and she got saved. I did not know her name. I saw her on board the *Carpathia*, but I forgot to ask her name. There were also two Swedes, and a first-class passenger—I believe that is what he said—and he had just his underwear on. I asked him if he was married, and he said he had a wife and a child. There was also a fireman named Thompson on the same raft. He had burned one of his hands. Also there was a young boy, with a name that sounded like Volunteer. He was at St. Vincent's Hospital afterwards. Thompson was there, too.

The next morning we could see some of the lifeboats. One of the boats had a sail up, and he came pretty close, and then we said, "One, two, three"; we said that quite often. We did not talk very much, except that we would say, "One, two, three," and scream together for help.

Senator Smith: Was this collapsible boat that you were in filling with water?

Mr. Abelseth: There was water on the top.

Senator Smith: Were you on the top of the overturned collapsible boat?

Mr. Abelseth: No. The boat was not capsized. We were standing on the deck. In this little boat the canvas was not raised up. We tried to raise the canvas up but we could not get it up. We stood all night in about 12 or 14 inches of water on this thing and our feet were in the water all the time. I could not say exactly how long we were there, but I know it was more than four hours on this raft.

This same boat I was telling about—

Senator Smith: The sailboat [the lifeboat with its sail up; No. 14]?

Mr. Abelseth: Yes; when the *Carpathia* came she was picked up. There were several boats there then. It was broad daylight and you could see the *Carpathia*. Then this boat sailed down to us and took us aboard, and took us in to the *Carpathia*. I helped row in to the *Carpathia*.

Senator Smith: Did you see any icebergs on that morning?

Mr. Abelseth: We saw three big ones. They were quite a ways off.

Senator Smith: I want to direct your attention again to the steerage. Do you think the passengers in the steerage and in the bow of the boat had an opportunity to get out and up on the decks, or were they held back?

Mr. Abelseth: Yes, I think they had an opportunity to get up.

Senator Smith: There were no gates or doors locked, or anything that kept them down?

Mr. Abelseth: No, sir; not that I could see.

Senator Smith: You said that a number of them climbed up one of these cranes?

Mr. Abelseth: That was on the top, on the deck; after they got on the deck. That was in order to get up on this boat deck.

Senator Smith: Onto the top deck?

Mr. Abelseth: Onto the top deck; yes. But down where we were, in the rooms, I do not think there was anybody that held anybody back.

Senator Smith: You were not under any restraint? You were permitted to go aboard the boats the same as other passengers?

Mr. Abelseth: Yes, sir.

Senator Smith: Do you think the steerage passengers in your part of the ship all got out?

Mr. Abelseth: I could not say that for sure; but I think the most of them got out.

Senator Smith: Did that part of the ship fill rapidly with water?

Mr. Abelseth: Oh, yes; I think that filled up; yes. There was a friend of mine told me that he went back for something he wanted, and then there was so much water there that he could not get to his room.

Senator Smith: Were the three relatives of yours from Norway lost?

Mr. Abelseth: Yes; they were lost.

Senator Smith: You never saw them after you parted from them at the time you spoke of?

Mr. Abelseth: No, sir.

Senator Smith: Do you know how many people there were in that lifeboat that you were in?

Mr. Abelseth: I could not say for sure; but there must have been 10 or 12. They got saved off of this raft. There was one man from New Jersey that I came in company with from London. I do not know what his name was. I tried to keep this man alive; but I could not make it. It was just at the break of day, and he was lying down, and he seemed to be kind of unconscious; he was not really dead, and I took him by the shoulder and raised him up, so that he was sitting up on this deck.

Senator Smith: He was sitting on a seat?

Mr. Abelseth: He was just sitting down right on the deck. I said to him, "We can see a ship now. Brace up." And I took one of his hands and raised it up like that [illustrating], and I took him by the shoulder and shook him, and he said, "Who are you?" He said, "Let me be. Who are you?" I held him up like that for a while, but I got tired and cold, and I took a little piece of a small board, a lot of which were floating around there, and laid it under his head on the edge of the boat to keep his head from the water; but it was not more than about half an hour or so when he died.

Senator Smith: That is all. We are very much obliged to you.

American Inquiry, 1035–1040

CHAPTER 5

"Make Your Ship as Unsinkable as You Can"

While we are considering reversible opinions and doubtful judgments, and the matters of life and death that may depend on them, let us look at the most notorious example of the *Titanic*'s alleged moral failure—her neglect to carry enough lifeboats for all on board.

If there is blame here, there is blame enough to gratify all tastes. Enemies of corporate greed can say that accommodations for 1,178 out of a possible 3,547 people (of whom, luckily, *Titanic* was carrying only about 2,200) look like a bad joke. Enemies of government regulation can reply that the British Board of Trade required an even less handsome provision of 962 spaces. But people on each side will be left to wonder what White Star and the Board of Trade could possibly have had in mind.

One thing they had in mind was keeping costs as low as possible. As churlish as it may seem to mention this, even lifesaving equipment can, at some point, have a prohibitive cost. Lord Mersey asked, rhetorically, "If vessels are made by different devices so secure that they cease to be commercially valuable, they cease to go to sea at all?" The answer is "yes."[54] But lifeboats did not represent a major cost; nor was the space required for lifeboats an indispensable commercial asset. The *Titanic*'s designers provided every class of passengers with

16. *Titanic's boat deck: How many boats for how many passengers? Courtesy of the Mariners' Museum, Newport News, Virginia.*

advantages much costlier than lifeboats, and not all of these advantages were strictly necessary to attract customers. Lifeboats didn't particularly hurt the balance sheet, and they didn't particularly help it, either. People didn't decide either to use or not to use a vessel because of its ratio of lifeboat spaces to passengers.

Yet the most basic question has nothing to do with money. It is, How many lifeboats are required to make a ship "secure"? To put this in another way, How many lifeboats can it use effectively? If you ask questions like that about the *Titanic*, the answer seems, at first, straightforward: Enough lifeboats to carry everyone on board. The *Titanic* disaster was, in its way, ideal. The weather was perfectly calm, and the ship took a fairly long time to sink, as sinkings in mid-ocean go. In the words of a survivor, "she took two hours and forty minutes . . . and that's an awful long time."[55] There was time to launch twice as many boats, if they had only been provided.

But this fact, like so many other facts about the night of April 14–15, can be delusive. It can lead to judgments about "security" that are far too easy.

When water finally washed over the *Titanic's* upper decks, she had not succeeded in launching all her boats. Out of the original complement of four collapsibles and 16 wooden lifeboats, two collapsibles remained. The *Titanic* literally could not have used any more lifeboats, primarily because her boat crews were not organized well enough to save time by launching a number of them simultaneously.[56] And nature is much less susceptible to organization than a ship's crew. Weather on the North Atlantic is seldom calm, and if a ship is going to sink, it may well develop a list so severe that lifeboats on one side cannot be lowered, because they will hit the hull, and lifeboats on the other side cannot be loaded, because they are swinging too far from the deck. If there is any sea running, boats can probably be launched only on the lee side, so "boats for all" will mean boats for all on *each* side of the ship.

No large liner has ever seriously tried to satisfy this both-sides-of-the-ship criterion; lifeboats simply take up too much room. The less demanding (but often barely meaningful) standard is boats for all, located *somewhere* on the ship—a standard that the *Titanic* could have satisfied. Arrangements could have been made to store, stack, or "nest" lifeboats on deck, or to reach the required number of "lifeboat" spaces by substituting rafts and collapsibles for some of the ordinary wooden boats. These were the methods employed on other ships in the aftermath of the *Titanic* disaster.

But although rafts and collapsibles are smaller and more storable than wooden lifeboats, they are very much less seaworthy. They can also be hard to launch; but then again, so can wooden lifeboats. Massive and unwieldy, they have to be lowered (in the evacuation of a ship like the *Titanic*) a distance of seven stories, "filled with people who are not 'boatwise,'" to quote the contemptuous expression of *Titanic*'s Second Officer, Charles Lightoller.[57] As the number of boats increases, so does the difficulty of working with them; and any lifeboat is a dangerous thing to work with. When there are serious time constraints, or a heavy list, the results are pretty much what you would expect. The Cunard liner *Lusitania*, which was torpedoed in 1915, sank in only 18 minutes. The scene of horror was rendered yet more horrible by lifeboats crashing into the ship, the sea, and crowds of passengers.[58]

"In disasters of this kind time is an important factor." That is the modest generalization of *The Marine Engineer and Naval Architect* (September 1912), commenting on the *Titanic* disaster. There may be sufficient boats, but there must also be sufficient time to launch them. According to the expert calculations of 1912, boats on troop ships could be loaded at a maximum rate of 1,100 people per hour.[59] If the *Titanic*'s passengers and crew had been soldiers on a troop ship, such a feat of organization could, theoretically, have saved them all, with half an hour to spare; the *Titanic* took a long time to sink. But an injury that will sink a ship is often the kind of injury that will sink her right away, meanwhile hindering and delaying attempts to lower her boats.

Severe weather or a disastrous fire can present conditions much less favorable to evacuation than steady leakage from iceberg wounds. If a very large ocean liner is in serious distress, it is unlikely that everyone will escape simply by using her boats. In an eerie footnote to the *Titanic* story, the *Britannic*, her posthumous sister, made a close approach to the ideal. When her bow exploded, the *Britannic* was carrying only around 1,100 people, about the number of people who could have fitted into the *Titanic*'s lifeboats, if they had all been filled. The *Britannic*'s crew made better use of her boats. Operating under military conditions, they approximated the top speed that had been estimated for a military evacuation. In the 55 minutes that the *Britannic* took to sink, nearly everyone escaped in 35 lifeboats. Only 30 people perished, most of them killed when their lifeboats were sucked into the ship's propellers.[60]

Less ideal, but easier to foretell, was what happened aboard the *Andrea Doria*. Like every other post-*Titanic* ocean liner, the *Doria* carried lifeboats for all; but after she was injured in a collision in 1956, she listed so badly that few of them could be used effectively. During the hours that passed between the accident and her sinking, 97 percent of the people on board were saved—mainly because other ships soon arrived and transferred passengers with their own boats.[61]

In 1912, lifeboats were valued chiefly for their ability to ferry a few people at a time from a distressed liner to a rescue ship, which would use its own boats to speed the operation. The point was to build liners that would stay afloat until help arrived. The idea that every great liner should function as "its own lifeboat" was sensible and widely shared. It was a reason for the apparently bizarre regulatory system commonly in use, in which the required number of lifeboat accommodations was based on the tonnage of ships, not on the number of people they carried. The largest liners had the best chance of staying afloat for the longest time, so they could do with a smaller proportion of lifeboat spaces than other vessels. Considering the dangers of decks overcrowded with "lifesaving" equipment, it was thought that liners that could carry several thousand people probably *should* not have boats for all.

That was the reasoning. Even after the *Titanic* disaster, the editor of *Scientific American* published a book called *An Unsinkable Titanic,* in which he emphasized the hazards of relying on lifeboats and argued that unsinkability should continue to be the goal.[62] During the British *Titanic* inquiry, Attorney-General Isaacs took it for granted that "it is much more important to make your ship as near as unsinkable as you can than to provide boats," and Lord Mersey answered, "Of course it is."[63] That exchange reflected the wisdom of shipowners and regulators almost everywhere. It probably reflected the wisdom of sailors, too. Lightoller was an exception, at least in retrospect. Two decades after his bad experience with the *Titanic,* he recorded his opinion that Mersey's inquiry had been a "whitewash" of "the utter inadequacy of the lifesaving equipment then prevailing." But he also declared that "the pendulum has swung to the other extreme and the margin of safety reached the ridiculous."[64] One cannot know for sure where he wanted the pendulum to stop, or where, indeed, it ought to have stopped.

What is clear is the fact that efforts to increase the margin of safety are not cost-free; they can easily have tragic as well as "ridiculous" results. One highly acclaimed product of post-*Titanic* anxieties about maritime safety regulation was the La Follette Seamen's Act of 1915, named for William Alden Smith's fellow midwestern Progressive, Senator Robert La Follette (Republican, Wisconsin). The act required, among other things, that more crewmen of particular classifications be engaged to handle lifeboats on American passenger ships. As soon as the act became effective, the costs of implementing it started to put American ships out of business in the trans-Pacific passenger trade. But a still larger disaster would result from the act's requirement for additional boats and rafts on Great Lakes steamers.[65]

Because the routes followed by these ships brought them into very frequent contact with one another, it had been argued that there was little need for them to carry large fleets of lifeboats. If one ship got into trouble, others would come along to take off the passengers. The argument had also been made that Great Lakes vessels tended to be of shallower draft than ocean-going vessels; increasing the weight of boats and rafts on their upper decks might cause them to capsize. Such arguments were swept aside, and the act was passed.

In mid-1915, the owners of the *Eastland*, a large Lake Michigan passenger steamer, added a number of boats and rafts to her top deck. This life-saving equipment represented partial satisfaction of the provisions of the Seamen's Act, set to come into force later that year. On the morning of July 24, 1915, three weeks after the additions were completed, a crowd of factory workers on their way to a company picnic boarded the *Eastland* at her dock in the Chicago River. The ship promptly capsized, killing 844 people, 841 of them passengers, slightly more than the number of passengers who were lost with the *Titanic*. The *Eastland*'s lifeboats were never used, but they were a crucial cause of the disaster.[66]

None of the problems considered in this chapter had any effect on public opinion, the authority to which Lord Mersey bowed when he finally recommended the requirement of lifeboats for all.[67] It was an authority to which trans-Atlantic shipowners had already bowed. So far as this authority was concerned, the provision of boats for all was a risk-free moral necessity. The decision to provide them may have been right, as, on balance, I think it was, if only because passengers henceforth expected "lifeboats for all" and would presumably panic at any rumor that a vessel in distress (however minor) failed to meet the technical standard. Anxiety about the number of lifeboats is a tribute to the power of the *Titanic* story, in one of its interpretations. But the issue was never as simple as the public thought. Like some of the other morally fraught decisions I have mentioned, the requirement of lifeboats for all represented a juggling with risks, risks that were no more calculable after the *Titanic* disaster than they were before it.

"There Was a Lot of Pathos . . . of Course"

Testimony of Mrs. J. Stuart White, a Disgruntled Passenger in Lifeboat No. 8

Senator Smith: Do you make the Waldorf-Astoria your permanent home, Mrs. White?

Mrs. White: My home really is Briarcliffe Lodge; Briarcliff [sic] Manor, N.Y. That is my summer home. When I am in New York, I am always here at the Waldorf-Astoria.

Senator Smith: I want to ask you one or two questions, Mrs. White, and let you answer them in your own way. You were a passenger on the *Titanic*?

Mrs. White: Yes. . . . I remained in my room until I came out that night [Sunday, April 14]. . . .

Senator Smith: Were you aroused especially by the impact?

Mrs. White: No; not at all. I was just sitting on the bed, just ready to turn the lights out. It did not seem to me that there was any very great impact at all. It was just as though we went over about a thousand marbles. There was nothing terrifying about it at all.

Senator Smith: Were you aroused by any one of the ship's officers or crew?

Mrs. White: No.

Senator Smith: Do you know whether there was any alarm turned in for the passengers?

Mrs. White: We heard no alarm whatever. We went immediately on deck ourselves. . . .

Senator Smith: Where did you enter the lifeboat [No. 8]?

Mrs. White: I entered the lifeboat from the top deck, where the boats were. We had to enter the boat there. There was no other deck to the steamer except the top deck. It was a perfect rat trap. There was no other deck that was open, at all. . . .

Senator Smith: Did you see anything after the accident bearing upon the discipline of the officers or crew, or their conduct, which you desire to speak of?

Mrs. White: Yes; lots about them.

Senator Smith: Tell me about that.

Mrs. White: For instance, before we cut loose from the ship two of the seamen with us—the men, I should say; I do not call them seamen; I think they were dining-room stewards—before we were cut loose from the ship they took out cigarettes and lighted them; on an occasion like that! That is one thing that we saw. All of those men escaped under the pretense of being oarsmen. The man who rowed me took his oar and rowed all over the boat, in every direction. I said to him, "Why don't you put the oar in the oarlock?" He said, "Do you put it in that hole?" I said, "Certainly." He said, "I never had an oar in my hand before." I spoke to the other man and he said, "I have never had an oar in my hand before, but I think I can row." Those were the men that we were put to sea with at night—with all those magnificent fellows left on board, who would have been such a protection to us. Those were the kind of men with whom we were put out to sea that night. . . .

Everybody knew we were in the vicinity of icebergs. Even in our staterooms it was so cold that we could not leave the port hole open. It was terribly cold. I made the remark to Miss Young, on Sunday morning: "We must be very near icebergs to have such cold weather as this." It was unusually cold.

It was a careless, reckless thing. It seems almost useless to speak of it.

No one was frightened on the ship. There was no panic. I insisted on Miss Young getting into something warm, and I got into something warm, and we locked our trunks and bags and went on deck.

There was no excitement whatever. Nobody seemed frightened. Nobody was panic-stricken. There was a lot of pathos when husbands and wives kissed each other good-by, of course.

We were the second boat pushed away from the ship, and we saw nothing that happened after that. We were not near enough. We heard the yells of the steerage passengers as they went down, but we saw none of the harrowing part of it at all.

As I have said before, the men in our boat were anything but seamen, with the exception of one man. The women all rowed, every one of them. Miss Young rowed every minute. The men could not row. They did not know the first thing about it. Miss Swift, from Brooklyn, rowed every minute, from the steamer to the *Carpathia*. Miss Young rowed every minute, also, except when she was throwing up, which she did six or seven times. Countess Rothe[s] stood at the tiller. Where would we have been if it had not been for our women, with such men as that put in charge of the boat? Our head seaman would give an order and those men who knew nothing about the handling of a boat would say, "If you don't stop talking through that hole in your face there will be one less in the boat." We were in the hands of men of that kind. I settled two or three fights between them, and quieted them down. Imagine getting right out there and taking out a pipe and filling it and standing there smoking, with the women rowing, which was most dangerous; we had woolen rugs all around us.

Another thing which I think is a disgraceful point. The men were asked, when they got into our boat, if they could row. Imagine asking men that who are supposed to be at the head of lifeboats—imagine asking them if they can row.

There is another point that has never been brought out in regard to this accident and that is that that steamer had no open decks except the top deck. How could they fill the lifeboats properly? They could not lower a lifeboat 70 feet with any degree of safety with more than 20 people in it. Where were they going to get any more in them on the way down? There were no other open decks.

Just to think that on a beautiful starlit night—you could see the stars reflected in the water—with all those Marconi warnings, that they would allow such an accident to happen, with such a terrible loss of life and property.

It is simply unbearable, I think. . . .

I never saw a finer body of men in my life than the men passengers on this trip—athletes and men of sense—and if they had been permitted to enter these lifeboats with their families the boats would have been appropriately manned and many more lives saved, instead of allowing the stewards to get in the boats and save their lives, under the pretense that they could row, when they knew nothing whatever about it.

American Inquiry, 1005–1007, 1009–1010

"Away for an Hour or So"

Testimony of Thomas Jones, Able Seaman in Charge of Lifeboat No. 8

Senator Newlands: Did you think at that time it would be as safe to stay on the ship as to go in the boat?

Mr. Jones: I thought they were only sending us away for an hour or so, until they got squared up again.

Senator Newlands: Until they got what?

Mr. Jones: Until they got her pumped out.

Senator Newlands: Can you give us the names of any passengers on your boat?

Mr. Jones: One lady. She had a lot to say, and I put her to steering my boat.

Senator Newlands: What was her name?

Mr. Jones: Lady Rothe[s]. She was a countess or something.

American Inquiry, 572

CHAPTER 6

"It Would Have Been Outrageously Bad Seamanship"

Juggling with risks can have strange effects on moral judgment. Risks can be juggled away as if they had no weight at all; or they can become the focus of attention, until all that people can see is the heavy objects that keep landing in both their hands.

The first of those two effects appeared in the American public's response to Bruce Ismay's moral problem. Before the *Titanic* disaster, it was universally agreed that the managers of a steamship company had no business interfering with the management of the ships themselves. The risk was too high. (Given Ismay's ignorance of navigation, it was stupendously high.) There would also, quite obviously, be heavy risks involved if a corporate official tried to assume responsibility for the evacuation of a ship. Such a person could easily do more harm than good.

As it happened, Ismay assumed none of these risks. When he was handed the iceberg warning on April 14, he did not advise Captain Smith to slow down. When the *Titanic* was sinking, Ismay helped other people enter the lifeboats, but he felt no duty to manage the operation or to go down with the ship as a consequence of his management responsibility. He acted like an ordinary passenger and entered a lifeboat when he saw no other passengers competing for the space. But popular opinion

17. First Officer William Murdoch: Attempting to swing the *Titanic* away from the iceberg, he accomplished her destruction. *Courtesy of the Mariners' Museum, Newport News, Virginia.*

noticed only the fact that Ismay failed to make the *Titanic* slow down and failed to make sure that his fellow-passengers escaped. It took no account of the risks that he (and everyone else) would have run if he had tried to take charge.

Lord Mersey and his investigators experienced the second effect of a juggling with risks. They never lost sight of the risks inherent in any decision, including the risk of pronouncing moral judgment. Sometimes, they were simply mesmerized by the risks appearing on either hand. They were particularly impressed by the strange case of the *Titanic's* swerve.

When the lookouts told First Officer Murdoch that there was an iceberg right ahead, Murdoch turned the ship to port; and *Titanic*, as I have said, nearly missed the iceberg. She did miss the violence of a head-on collision. But testimony showed that if Murdoch had decided to hit the berg head-on, *Titanic* would have repeated the famous experience of the *Arizona:* her bow would have crumpled, but her bulkheads would have held.

She would not have received the fatal wounds to her starboard side. She would have remained afloat. Even Ismay knew that. The 200 people who were sleeping closest to the bow would have died; but that would have been many fewer people than the 1,500 who did die.[68]

One could easily conclude that the ideal officer would have calculated the risk of trying to swerve and the risk of not trying to swerve (the iceberg is close, the ship is heavy, the force of any collision will be tremendous), and would have decided to hold his course. No one, however, would have hailed such a person as the savior of 1,500 innocent people. Instead, everyone would have damned him as the murderer of 200 innocent people.

This problem tormented Mersey and his assistants. They did not know what to do with it. Attorney-General Isaacs tried going at it head-on. He said that if a liner were purposely driven into the ice, "I hope I am not on it, that is all." White Star's counsel Robert Finlay was determined to have things both ways, and in the strongest terms. He argued that "it would have been outrageously bad seamanship" for Murdoch *not* to have swerved, even though, "as things turned out," what he did "was unfortunate—most unfortunate." Mersey conceded that Murdoch exercised "good seamanship." Still, he reflected, if Murdoch had held his course he "would have saved the ship." Like White Star's lawyer, Mersey was juggling madly; but he was by no means happy with his act. Finally even he surrendered:

> It is not worth while discussing it. Have we got anything to do with it? We are all agreed that Murdoch was quite right in doing what he did.[69]

That was that. Yet Mersey was not just trying to escape. He was being very careful. He had been thinking about the relationship between risk and moral responsibility. He was aware that his own inquiry could change that relationship. A running of risks that was quite innocent *before* the disaster might now, with improved awareness of one set of possible consequences, transform itself into "negligence of a very gross kind."[70]

That is what Mersey thought about Captain Smith's way of dealing with the risks of ice and speed. Of this, Mersey would write:

> I am not able to blame Captain Smith. He had not the experience which his own misfortune has afforded to those whom he has left behind, and he was doing only that which other skilled men would have done in the same position.

Still,

> What was a mistake in the case of the "Titanic" would without doubt be negligence in any similar case in the future.[71]

But Mersey was not prepared to tell seamen that they should take the risk of running their vessels into icebergs. Who knows what the result of such advice would be? Perhaps it would be some misfortune about which later investigators would write an instructive story. Mersey let that alone; *he* was too careful to run such risks. And yet, as he said, "a man may make, as we all know, a mistake which is due sometimes even to too great care."[72] The risks remained heavy on both his hands.

But how should one regard the too great care exercised by Captain Stanley Lord, master of the steamship *Californian* and provider of yet another strange episode in the *Titanic* story? Here was risk management—prudent, sober, perhaps even conscientious—but neither Mersey nor any of the other investigators was of two minds about it.

The *Californian* was a vessel of the Leyland line. It was owned, ironically, by the same Morgan holding company that owned White Star. On April 14, the *Californian* encountered field ice and stopped for the night. Another ship appeared in the vicinity and started firing rockets. Lord received reports about them, but he neglected to awaken his wireless operator to find out whether anything was wrong. Lord was sleepy, too; and he was concerned about the light ice that was bumping against his ship. The *Californian* sat still until morning. Then Lord had

18. Captain Stanley Lord of the *Californian:* After his involvement, or (as he suggested) his non-involvement with the *Titanic,* he lost his job and much of his reputation. Attempts to vindicate him still go on. *Courtesy of the Mariners' Museum, Newport News, Virginia.*

one of his officers wake up the wireless operator, who immediately discovered that the *Titanic* had foundered. Lord got the *Californian* going and maneuvered through the ice until he arrived, several hours too late, at the site of *Titanic*'s wreck. He kept all mention of rockets out of his log, and he hoped that no one would be the wiser.

Regrettably for Captain Lord, stories from two of his crewmen got into the American press, and he was left to explain himself, somehow. He suggested that the *Titanic* was not visible
from the *Californian*. It might have been *some other ship* that
was firing rockets—which, as he preferred to think, were some
shipping company's communications signals. These suggestions
made people wonder why Captain Lord had not done his best
to find out what was going on with that *other* ship.[73] Some may
also have wondered why the rockets of the other ship, coming
as they did from the general direction of the *Titanic*, were not
noticed on the *Titanic* herself, where anxious observers would
have welcomed any sign of life in the surrounding ocean.

The real explanation, as Attorney-General Isaacs surmised,[74]
was that Captain Lord, meeting field ice for the first time in his
career, had decided that he did not want to test his own ship
against the unaccustomed risk. It is possible that Lord was hes-
itant to rouse his wireless operator because he did not want to
confirm the fact that another vessel was in distress and find himself obligated to do something about it. He weighed the risks,
both from ice and from moral responsibility, and he tried to
reduce them to the lowest possible level.

For this he was censured by Lord Mersey and Senator Smith,
and he was fired by the Leyland line, which discovered that his
inordinate skill at risk management had made him a distinct liability to public relations. Six months after his firing, he was
offered a job by the Nitrate Producers Steamship Company, for
which he would eventually command a ship larger than the
Californian. He retired in 1928, when he was only 50 years old,
and spent many comfortable years reading good books. In
1958, he happened to see the notice of a movie, *A Night to
Remember,* that implied criticism of his actions in regard to the
Titanic. He then appealed for vindication to the secretary of his
professional group, the Mercantile Marine Service Association,
who took up his cause. Since that time, people interested in the
Titanic have hotly debated the nature of the decisions that Lord
made, or evaded, on the night of her distress. An influential

19. Captain Arthur Rostron of the *Carpathia:* Informed by his wireless operator that the *Titanic* was in trouble, Rostron immediately changed course, made all the speed he could, arranged for the deployment of every possible kind of rescue equipment, and ordered up a lot of coffee. *Courtesy of the Mariners' Museum, Newport News, Virginia.*

party of researchers is convinced, as Lord obviously convinced himself, that when the facts are viewed dispassionately they will demonstrate that his judgment was correct by normal standards of seamanship.

But suppose they won't. Suppose we accept the conventional view that Lord simply neglected to intervene in a situation that might have posed a danger to his ship. Lurking near that hypothesis is yet another glittering fact that can suddenly reverse itself and become a hazardous black berg. Why is it, one may ask, that Captain Lord of the *Californian* was blamed for his moral irresponsibility, while Captain Rostron of the *Carpathia* was honored, for his moral heroism, with a gold medal from Congress, the command of the great liners *Mauretania* and *Berengaria*, and the applause of the whole world?

The reply, of course, is that Rostron fulfilled the sailor's traditional notion of duty. Lightoller stated it in this way: "Absolutely no effort shall be spared in an endeavor to save life at sea. A man must even be prepared to hazard his ship and his life."[75] But it might be argued that Lord also had a responsibility, the responsibility not to risk his ship and the lives of his crew unnecessarily. So he didn't. But Rostron took that risk, and more: Lord's ship carried no passengers; Rostron's carried almost 800. Would Rostron have become the hero of April 15, 1912, if he had driven the *Carpathia* at full speed onto one of the icebergs that littered her path? *Should* Rostron have become a hero for assuming such a serious risk, while Lord was denounced for refusing it? Perhaps public opinion was wrong again.

Once you reach this longitude, the sky darkens and the ocean fills with ice. There is danger here, the danger of losing all memory of what morality is. To avert disaster, we will have to make a hard turn to starboard and try to find another course.

"That Is All Right"

Testimony of John Collins, Assistant Cook

Mr. Collins: [T]he ship struck the iceberg, and it wakened me. I put on my trousers, got out of bed, and they were letting off steam in the stoke hole [hold]. I asked what was the matter, and it seemed she struck an iceberg. The word came down the alleyway that there was no harm, and everyone returned to their bunks. . . . I put on my trousers and went up on to the deck, up forward, and I saw the deck almost packed with ice on the starboard side. . . .

I went back into the bedroom and was told to lie down, and I got up again. I did not take off any of my clothes, and I came out again and saw the stewards in their white jackets in the passageway; the passengers were running forward, the stewards were steering them, and they made a joke of it, and we all turned in then and the word came in that we were to get out of our beds and get the life belts on and get up to the upper deck. . . .

We went up to the deck when the word came. Then I met a companion of mine, a steward, and I asked him what number my boat was, and he said No. 16; so I went up to No. 16 boat, and I seen both firemen and sailors with their bags ready for No. 16 boat. I said to myself, "There is no chance there," and I ran back to the deck, ran to the port side on the saloon deck [the boat deck] with another steward and a woman and two children, and the steward had one of the children in his arms and the woman was crying.

I took the child off of the woman and made for one of the boats. Then the word came around from the starboard side there was a collapsible boat [Collapsible A] getting launched on the starboard side and that all women and children were to make for it. So me and another steward and the two children and the woman came around on that side, the starboard side, and when we got around there we saw then that it was forward.

CHAPTER 7

· ·

"I Knew It Was My Duty"

At 12:00 A.M. on April 15, 1912, lookout Reginald Lee climbed down from the *Titanic*'s crow's nest. His ill-fated watch was over, and he went to his assigned lifeboat, No. 11. But instead of staying there, he started forward to work on the other boats. By the time he returned to No. 11, there was no room for him. Attorney-General Isaacs asked him if he had had "orders" to help with those boats, if he "had to do it." Lee replied, "I knew it was my duty, and that is why I went there. I did not have any orders myself." Lee went to assist with No. 13, was ordered into it, and was saved.[76]

Chief baker Charles Joughin was listed as the crewman who was supposed to enter boat No. 10 and take charge of it. But he busied himself by going downstairs to find more women and children, bringing them to the boat deck, and assisting or "throwing" them into the lifeboat. At 1:10, the lifeboat left without him. "Why," he was asked by one of Mersey's assistants, "did not you go, seeing that you were in charge?" "I would have set a bad example," he replied. After the departure of No. 10, Joughin went to his room and took a drink, evidently a nice long drink. When the *Titanic* sank, he was sufficiently fortified to ease off the stern and swim out to an overturned boat—Collapsible B, which had floated off the ship because

20. Harold Bride, the *Titanic*'s surviving wireless operator, evacuates the *Carpathia* in New York harbor. On the night of April 14–15, Bride fought and probably killed a man, was washed off the *Titanic*'s deck, found his way onto an overturned lifeboat, clung to it for several hours with his feet in freezing water, and was rescued by the *Carpathia*. He spent the voyage to New York helping *Carpathia*'s exhausted wireless operator with the many messages he had to send. *Courtesy of the Mariners' Museum, Newport News, Virginia.*

there had not been enough time to launch it. The boat was in trouble and could not take him aboard, so he floated beside it until another boat picked him up. He was saved.[77]

At 2:05 A.M., while Captain Lord was sitting tight in the chartroom of the *Californian,* and the *Titanic* was lowering the last lifeboat that could be lowered, Captain Smith walked to the cabin on the boat deck where the young operators, Jack Phillips and Harold Bride, were sending distress calls. Smith told them, "You can do no more . . . You look out for yourselves." But, as Bride testified, "Mr. Phillips took the 'phones when the Captain had gone away and he started in to work again." The two boys kept working, and they kept writing their wireless log. Water was coming into the cabin. Bride went to the bedroom for a moment, and when he came back he found a crewman trying to steal Phillips's lifebelt. He and Phillips fought with the intruder and knocked him out. "I did my duty," Bride said. "I hope I finished him." The wireless boys sent their last message three minutes before the *Titanic* sank. Then they swam to the overturned lifeboat. They rode out the night on its wet, perilously balanced planks. Bride lived; Phillips died.[78]

None of the people in these stories was heedless of risks, but none of them equated moral responsibility with risk management. They were not self-sacrificing altruists. There were limits to what they would do for others. They would save themselves if they could. They might even kill to preserve their lives. But they measured risk to their lives against what was most valuable to them within their lives—a sense of duty. They would save their lives if they could do so and remain consistent with their other values. This, it appears, was their difference from Captain Lord, who took account of every risk except the risk of being the kind of person who cares only about the risks.

"Threw Them In"

Testimony of Charles Joughin, Chief Baker

Mr. Cotter [representing the National Union of Stewards]: You went up on deck?

Mr. Joughin: Yes.

Mr. Cotter: Your boat you told us was No. 10, and you were in charge?

Mr. Joughin: That is the one I was sent to.

Mr. Cotter: You said that boat was a yard and a half from the ship's side. Was there any difficulty in getting the women into that boat?

Mr. Joughin: Yes. That was through the list to port. Under ordinary conditions there would be no difficulty.

Mr. Cotter: But the boat was slung away from the ship through the list?

Mr. Joughin: Yes.

Mr. Cotter: Did you assist to get some women into the boat?

Mr. Joughin: I assisted to get most of them.

Mr. Cotter: You said you went down to the next deck to bring or try to force women up. Will you tell us—did you do that?

Mr. Joughin: Yes.

Mr. Cotter: Who did you bring up?

Mr. Joughin: I brought up two children and the mother—and a mother and a child, and other stewards were bringing up other women.

Mr. Cotter: What did you do with the children when you put them into the boat?

Mr. Joughin: Handed them into the boat or dropped them in.

Mr. Cotter: Threw them in?

Mr. Joughin: Threw them in.

Mr. Cotter: And what did you do with the mother?

Mr. Joughin: We wanted to throw her in, and I think she preferred to try and step in.

Mr. Cotter: What happened?

Mr. Joughin: She missed her footing.

Mr. Cotter: What happened then?

Mr. Joughin: This steward named Burke got hold of her foot and she swung head downwards for a few minutes, but she was got into B deck. Somebody caught her into B deck—no, A deck.

Mr. Cotter: Did you ever see her again?

Mr. Joughin: No.

Mr. Cotter: The children were saved?

Mr. Joughin: The children were saved.

Mr. Cotter: You said that you never went into your boat. Why did not you go, seeing that you were in charge?

Mr. Joughin: I would have set a bad example if I had jumped into the boat. None of the men felt inclined to get into the boat.

Mr. Cotter: You simply stood back to assist the women and children to get in?

Mr. Joughin: We stood back till the officers should give us the word, and we never got it, so that we never jumped for the boat.

Mr. Cotter: When you found your boat had gone you said you went down below. What did you do when you went down below?

Mr. Joughin: I went to my room for a drink.

Mr. Cotter: Drink of what?

Mr. Joughin: Spirits.

Lord Mersey: Does it very much matter what it was?

Mr. Cotter: Yes, my Lord, this is very important, because I am going to prove, or rather my suggestion is, that he then saved his life. I think his getting a drink had a lot to do with saving his life.

Mersey: He told you he had one glass of liqueur.

Mr. Cotter: Yes. (To the Witness) What kind of a glass was it?

Mr. Joughin: It was a tumbler half-full.

Mr. Cotter: A tumbler half-full of liqueur?

Mr. Joughin: Yes. . . .

The Solicitor-General: Can you tell us what happened to you?

Mr. Joughin: Yes, I eventually got on to the starboard side of the poop. . . .

The Solicitor-General: So that the rail was between you and the deck?

Mr. Joughin: Yes.

The Solicitor-General: Then what happened?

Mr. Joughin: Well, I was just wondering what next to do. I had tightened my belt and I had transferred some things out of this pocket into my stern pocket. I was just wondering what next to do when she went.

The Solicitor-General: And did you find yourself in the water?

Mr. Joughin: Yes. . . .

Mr. Cotter: She simply glided away?

Mr. Joughin: She went down that fashion. (*Showing.*) It was a glide. There was no great shock, or anything.

Mr. Cotter: She simply glided away?

Mr. Joughin: She simply glided away.

Mr. Cotter: When you got into the water and had swum to the collapsible boat you were pushed off, you say?

Mr. Joughin: Yes.

Mr. Cotter: Who pushed you off?

Mr. Joughin: I do not know.

Mr. Cotter: Did you say anything when you were pushed off?

Mr. Joughin: No.

Mr. Cotter: You made no statement to anyone?

Mr. Joughin: No.

Mr. Cotter: What condition were you in when you got to the "Carpathia"?

Mr. Joughin: I was all right barring my feet; they were swelled.

Mr. Cotter: Were you able to walk up the ladder?

Mr. Joughin: No.

Mr. Cotter: How did you get up?

Mr. Joughin: On my knees.

British Inquiry, 145, 142, 145

CHAPTER 8

"What Was It You Were Afraid Of?"

One may think ill of Captain Lord, but he is a sympathetic character compared to some of the people aboard the *Titanic*—or, more properly, some of the people who had been aboard the *Titanic* but had been lucky enough to find places in her lifeboats. The moral conduct of people in the boats was not something that either Senator Smith or Lord Mersey set out to analyze. Smith was more interested in discovering lapses in corporate morality; Mersey was more interested in understanding the technical details of the disaster itself. But neither of them could restrain his curiosity, and the testimony of the boats is on record. The record is very mixed.

When the *Titanic* sank, hundreds of people were swept off her decks into the freezing water. Upheld by their lifebelts, they were slowly dying of exposure. They were screaming for help; the noise was terrible. In some lifeboats, passengers or crewmen, or both, decided that they should help. Lifeboat No. 4, loaded with wealthy women, was one of the last to escape from the *Titanic*. But when the ship sank, No. 4 turned and began to rescue people: "Some of the women protested, but others persisted, and we dragged in six or seven men." They picked up people crying in the water until no more cries were heard.[79]

In boat No. 14, Officer Lowe gathered volunteers from other boats and steered toward the people in the water,

91

although he waited to do so until (in his brutal way of putting it) "the drowning people had thinned out."[80] By the time that happened, he was able to pick up only four people, one of whom did not survive.

> **Senator Smith:** And you picked up how many?
> **Frank Evans [able seaman]:** We picked up four persons alive.
> **Senator Smith:** Any dead?
> **Mr. Evans:** One died on the way back, sir. There were plenty of dead bodies about us.
> **Senator Smith:** How many? Scores of them?
> **Mr. Evans:** You couldn't hardly count them, sir. I was afraid to look over the sides because it might break my nerves down.

> **Senator Duncan Fletcher [Democrat, Florida]:** You were then with Lowe in his boat and went back to where the *Titanic* sank?
> **Edward Buley [able seaman]:** Yes, sir; and picked up the remaining live bodies.
> **Senator Fletcher:** How many did you get?
> **Mr. Buley:** There were not very many there. We got four of them. All the others were dead.
> **Senator Fletcher:** Were there many dead?
> **Mr. Buley:** Yes, sir; there were a good few dead, sir. Of course you could not discern them exactly on account of the wreckage; but we turned over several of them to see if they were alive. It looked as though none of them were drowned. They looked as though they were frozen. The life belts they had on were that much [indicating] out of the water, and their heads laid back, with their faces on the water, several of them. Their hands were coming up like that [indicating]. . . .
> **Senator Fletcher:** They were not, apparently, drowned?
> **Mr. Buley:** It looked as though they were frozen altogether, sir.[81]

Lowe thought he was morally right in waiting to go back. "I made the attempt, sir, as soon as any man could do so, and I am not scared of saying it."[82] But according to one account, he received a moral education, of a certain type, after he finally decided to go.

Mrs. Charlotte Collyer, a second-class passenger on the *Titanic,* told readers of the *Washington Post* that Lowe sighted a floating door and "lying upon it, face downward . . . a small Japanese. He had lashed himself with a rope to his frail raft, using the broken hinges to make the knots secure. As far as we could see, he was dead. The sea washed over him every time the door bobbed up and down, and he was frozen stiff." The young man failed to respond to shouts, and Lowe was ready to write him off. "What's the use?" he said. "He's dead, likely, and if he isn't there's others better worth saving than a Jap!" Lowe turned the boat; it began to leave. The race card had won the trick.

And yet . . . "he changed his mind and went back." He had the young man pulled into the lifeboat. The women rubbed his frozen body, and he opened his eyes. Soon he was taking an oar from a tired sailor.

> The Japanese . . . worked like a hero until we were finally picked up. I saw Mr. Lowe watching him in open-mouthed surprise.
> "By Jove!" muttered the officer, "I'm ashamed of what I said about the little blighter. I'd save the likes o' him six times over, if I got the chance."[83]

This story is insufficiently corroborated (though uncontradicted). At the least, however, it is the kind of story that people in 1912 considered instructive; and it remains instructive about who they were and what they thought was a good decision.

But many other stories that floated away from the *Titanic*'s wreck are instructive because they lack any happy ending and agreeable moral lesson. Most people in the *Titanic*'s lifeboats showed little inclination to row back and save anyone, even if they might have been close enough to do so, and even if they knew that their friends and relatives might be dying in the water.

Some of the boats were full, or (like Ismay's Collapsible C) nearly full; and some of the passengers in the less encumbered boats were clearly not prepared to think the situation through. Others, thinking very hard, might be wondering how long they would have to depend on the boats to save their own lives. They

21. A matter of viewpoint: Collapsible lifeboat D is seen approaching the *Carpathia*. How would this boat look if we didn't know we were seeing it from a rescue ship? Would it seem absurdly small and hopeless? How would it look receding from the *Titanic*'s deck? Or sighted by a swimmer in the night? *Courtesy of the Mariners' Museum, Newport News, Virginia.*

might understand that the wireless had been used to summon help; they might reflect on the fact that the disaster had occurred in the main Atlantic shipping lane, where even accidental help might be anticipated. They might also reflect on what could occur in a crowded lifeboat if no rescuers happened to arrive. There was no guarantee that a ship called *Carpathia* would steam up within a few hours and rescue them all. They didn't know that yet. Still, the sea was quiet, and there was space in the lifeboats, and a try could be made, could it not? While they were thinking, the screams went on.

Boat No. 8 was less than half full. Captain Smith had said that it should steer for a light that was visible, off in the distance, a light that presumably came from another ship (such as the *Californian*). The travelers in No. 8 rowed for an hour without making any noticeable progress toward the light. At that point, they did notice that the *Titanic* had gone down. They were a long way from the place where she sank, but they could hear cries coming from that direction. Thomas Jones, the only seaman in the group, suggested that they start rowing back. A handful of people agreed, including the Countess of Rothes, who was steering the boat. Most people did not agree; they decided that they should keep trying to obey the captain's order. Jones said, "Ladies, if any of us are saved, remember I wanted to go back. I would rather drown with them than leave them." No. 8 did not go back.[84]

Boat No. 5, commanded by Officer Pitman, had about 25 vacant spaces. But when Pitman proposed going back, his passengers (especially the ladies) objected that "it was a mad idea"; they would be "swamped." Pitman did not go back. He halted, listening to the cries until they gradually "died away." Senator Smith wanted to know what the cries were like.

> **Mr. Pitman:** Well, I can not very well describe it. I would rather you would not speak of it.
> **Senator Smith:** I realize that it is not a pleasant theme, and yet I would like to know whether these cries were general and in chorus, or desultory and occasional?

Mr. Pitman: There was a continual moan for about an hour.[85]

In some boats, almost any evasion was enough to prevent an attempt at rescue. Quartermaster Robert Hitchins, commanding boat No. 6, explained to Lord Mersey that he could not rescue any of the people crying in the water because he didn't know "what direction to take. . . . I had no compass." Mersey replied, "You had your ears. Could not you hear where these cries came from?" Hitchins's passengers had wanted to go back, but Hitchins had refused. He said "there was only a lot of stiffs there." The passengers rebelled; one of them, the now-famous Mrs. Margaret ("Molly") Brown, eventually threatened to throw Hitchins overboard. But by then it was too late.[86]

The most arresting non-rescue story is the little epic of lifeboat No. 1. It has an odd cast of characters. One of them is C.E.H. Stengel, a leather manufacturer from Newark, New Jersey. Stengel was quoted in the post-disaster press accounts as denouncing the *Titanic*'s "criminal carelessness," accusing Ismay of beating the women and children to one of the first lifeboats, and claiming that he himself (in case you were wondering) "was dragged on board the lifeboat after jumping into the sea." Stengel, whose boat left about half an hour before Ismay's, later testified before Senator Smith that he saw Ismay only once, early in the *Titanic*'s voyage, and that the only trouble that he (Stengel) had had about getting into a lifeboat was the result of his own nervousness. The railing on the boat deck was "rather high," so he "rolled" rather than jumped into No. 1.

> The officer then said, "That is the funniest sight I have seen tonight," and he laughed quite heartily. That rather gave me some encouragement. I thought perhaps it was not so dangerous as I imagined.[87]

Joining jolly Mr. Stengel in lifeboat No. 1 were two persons aptly named for the ludicrous parts they were about to play: Sir Cosmo Duff Gordon and his wife, Lady Duff Gordon, best known as "Lucile," a fashionable dress designer. Lady Duff Gordon would also tell post-*Titanic* stories. She would claim that she had suffered from an inexplicable nervousness about traveling on the ship, but because her husband offered to accompany her, she got up courage and went.[88] This experiment in decision-making sheds new light on the relationship between bravery and simple irrationality.

Besides Stengel and the two Duff Gordons, boat No. 1 contained Lady Duff Gordon's secretary, Miss Francatelli, one other passenger (male), and seven crewmen. It was not exactly filled. It could hold 40 people, but through the haste of the supervising officer it had been lowered with only 12. Stengel, however, formed the curious impression that No. 1 was at its "capacity."[89]

His shipmate, Sir Cosmo, suffered from a similarly erroneous perception. On entering No. 1, he somehow found his accommodations cramped. He told the British investigators that he had not realized "there was plenty of room in the boat for more people." There was too much gear in the boat for him to appreciate that. He admitted that it did occur to him "that people in the water could be saved by a boat," but it was evidently not *his* boat he was thinking of. The idea of personally trying to save anybody never crossed his mind. He was too busy worrying about his wife, who became violently seasick as soon as No. 1 touched the (absolutely calm) waters of the ocean: "We had had rather a serious evening, you know." Sir Cosmo noticed that someone was rowing the lifeboat, but he didn't know where, and he didn't know why, and he didn't care. He speculated that the rowers wanted to make enough noise to "stop the sound" of the dying.[90]

Crewman Charles Hendrickson testified that he suggested going back, but his suggestion was quashed by the Duff Gordons, or by Lady Duff Gordon and Miss Francatelli: "They were scared to go back for fear of being swamped." So Hendrickson stopped suggesting.

22. The British inquiry: Lord Mersey and his associates (exalted, right), witness on the stand (left of center), and the star of the proceedings, the *Titanic* (half-model, left). *Courtesy of the Mariners' Museum, Newport News, Virginia.*

> **Lord Mersey:** Then am I to understand that because two of the passengers said it would be dangerous you all kept your mouths shut and made no attempt to rescue anybody?
>
> **Mr. Hendrickson:** That is right, Sir.[91]

The only rescue that the crewmen of No. 1 attempted was the rescue of the Duff Gordons from the British inquiry. The crew's attachment to the Duff Gordon family had been improved by charitable contributions of £5 each, delivered by Sir Cosmo on the decks of the *Carpathia*. Most of the crew showed up to testify that *nobody* in No. 1 had wanted to go back. But why not?

> **Lord Mersey:** I want to know why? What was it that you were afraid of?
>
> **George Symons [crewman in charge of No. 1]:** I was not afraid of anything; I was only afraid of endangering the lives of the people I had in the boat.
>
> **Mersey:** How? What was the danger? The ship had gone to the bottom. She was no longer a danger. What were you afraid of?
>
> **Mr. Symons:** At that time the ship had only just disappeared.
>
> **Mersey:** Never mind, it had disappeared, and had gone down to the bottom, two miles down, or something like that. What were you afraid of?
>
> **Mr. Symons:** I was afraid of the swarming.
>
> **Mersey:** Of what?
>
> **Mr. Symons:** Of the swarming of the people—swamping the boat
>
> **Mersey:** That is it, that is what you were afraid of. You were afraid there were too many people in the water?
>
> **Mr. Symons:** Yes.
>
> **Mersey:** And that your boat would be swamped?
>
> **Mr. Symons:** Yes.
>
> **Mersey:** I am not satisfied at all.[92]

And no wonder. It would have been quite a job for anybody to crawl out of the freezing darkness into a lightly loaded boat standing high in the water, unless he had help from the people inside. Boat No. 1 could hardly have been swamped by the human "swarm"; it would have had plenty of time to turn back before it was engulfed.

23. Captain Smith looks down from the bridge during the *Titanic*'s stop at Queenstown, Ireland. In the emergency lifeboat hanging outboard next to the bridge, Sir Cosmo Duff Gordon and eleven other fortunate people escaped the ship. Its davits were then used to launch Bruce Ismay's boat. *Courtesy of the Mariners' Museum, Newport News, Virginia.*

But we have the testimony of the lifeboat's company, page after page in the British inquiry.

Thomas Scanlan [counsel for the National Sailors' and Firemen's Union]: It would have been quite a safe thing to have gone back?

Albert Horswill [able seaman]: Yes.

. . . **Mr. Scanlan:** Did it not occur to you that the proper thing to do under those circumstances was to row back?

Mr. Horswill: It would have been the proper thing to do, but I had to obey the orders of the coxswain of the boat, so it was no good my suggesting anything at all.

Mr. Scanlan: Had the coxswain on your boat said "Oh, we must not go back"?

Mr. Horswill: There was no conversation. I never heard any orders from the coxswain at all.

Mr. Scanlan: You must have been greatly touched when you heard those poor creatures screaming for help?

Mr. Horswill: Yes.

Mr. Scanlan: Did you suppress your feelings and say not a word to anybody?

Mr. Horswill: Yes, that is right. I hardly knew what I was doing at the time, and I did not suggest anything at all.

Mr. Scanlan: You had two ladies and three gentlemen in the boat?

Mr. Horswill: That is right, Sir.

Mr. Scanlan: Is this you[r] evidence, that they also suppressed their feelings, and said nothing?

Mr. Horswill: That is right. I did not hear them say anything.

Mr. Scanlan: Did it not occur to you that it was really an inhuman thing to leave those people to perish when you could have gone to their assistance and rescued some of them?

Mr. Horswill: It was inhuman.

Mr. Scanlan: It was an inhuman thing?

Mr. Horswill: Yes.

Mr. Scanlan: Did you feel it to be so at the time?

Mr. Horswill: I did feel it, Sir.

Mr. Scanlan: Why did not you say something to those passengers?

Mr. Horswill: I had to obey the orders of the coxswain of the boat. I was in the boat just the same as they were.

Lord Mersey: You will not get him away from that, you know.[93]

"I was only following orders" would become one of the great moral excuses of the twentieth century. But in Able Seaman Horswill's story, there were no orders. And neither was there an effective concept of moral duty.

> **Lord Mersey:** I do not understand your frame of mind. You were surprised that no one made the suggestion that your boat should go back?
> **Robert Pusey [fireman]:** Yes.
> **Mersey:** Then were you surprised that you did not make the suggestion?
> **Mr. Pusey:** No.
> **Mersey:** Then you were surprised that no one else made the suggestion, but you were not surprised that you did not make it?
> **Mr. Pusey:** No.
> **Mersey:** It is a curious state of mind . . . [94]

Even more curious was the continuing state of mind of Sir Cosmo Duff Gordon, whose testimony made him look so pathetic that Mersey begged his examiners not to press him too hard: "The witness's position is bad enough." Sir Cosmo was asked to comment on the proposition that, since he had thought it "natural" to contribute £35 to the crew of his lifeboat, he might have thought it "equally natural" to consider saving some other people from a horrible death. Again he said that the possibility hadn't occurred to him.[95]

There were certain things that Ismay had failed, somewhat mysteriously, to reflect upon. The mystery of Duff Gordon lay in his apparent decision not to reflect on anything. His choices, perhaps, had not been hard. Mersey could not chart the weird interior of Duff Gordon's mind; it seemed to have no features. He gave it up. A few months later, Duff Gordon wrote to George Symons to say that "the whole of the Inquiry showed how entirely unable Lord Mersey was to appreciate what the circumstances really were."[96]

"You Ought to Be Damn Glad"

Testimony of Daisy Minahan

I was asleep in stateroom C-78; I was awakened by the crying of a woman in the passageway. I roused my brother and his wife, and we began at once to dress. No one came to give us warning. We spent five minutes in dressing and went on deck to the port side. The frightful slant of the deck toward the bow of the boat gave us our first thought of danger.

An officer came and commanded all women to follow, and he led us to the boat deck on the starboard side. He told us there was no danger, but to get into a lifeboat as a precaution only. After making three attempts to get into boats, we succeeded in getting into lifeboat No. 14. The crowd surging around the boats was getting unruly.

Officers were yelling and cursing at men to stand back and let the women get into the boats. In going from one lifeboat to another we stumbled over huge piles of bread lying on the deck.

When the lifeboat was filled there were no seamen to man it. The officer in command of No. 14 called for volunteers in the crowd who could row. Six men offered to go. At times when we were being lowered we were at an angle of 45 degrees and expected to be thrown into the sea. As we reached the level of each deck men jumped into the boat until the officer threatened to shoot the next man who jumped. We landed in the sea and rowed to a safe distance from the sinking ship. The officer counted our number and found us to be 48. The officer commanded everyone to feel in the bottom of the boat for a light. We found none. Nor was there bread or water in the boat. The officer, whose name I learned afterwards to be Lowe, was continually making remarks such as, "A good song to sing would be, Throw Out the Life Line,"* and "I think the best thing for you women to do is to take a nap."

The *Titanic* was fast sinking. After she went down the cries were horrible. This was at 2:20 A.M. by a man's watch who stood next to me. At this time three other boats and ours kept together by being tied to each other. The cries continued to come over the water. Some of the women implored Officer Lowe, of No. 14, to divide his passengers among the three other boats and go back to rescue. His first answer to these requests was, "You ought to be damn glad you are here and have got your own life." After some time he was persuaded to do as he was asked. As I came up to him to be transferred to the other boat he said, "Jump, God damn you, jump." I had showed no hesitancy and was waiting only my turn. . . .

It was just 4 o'clock when we sighted the *Carpathia*, and we were three hours getting to her. On the *Carpathia* we were treated with every kindness and given every comfort possible.

American Inquiry, 1104–1105

*A popular gospel song by Edwin Smith Ufford:

Soon will the season of rescue be o'er,
Soon will they drift to eternity's shore;
Haste, then, my brother, no time for delay,
But throw out the life-line and save them today.

CHAPTER 9

"Spectators of a Drama"

Whatever one thinks of Sir Cosmo Duff Gordon (and I don't think very much of him), one may still ask questions about the standard of duty that he failed to honor. The questions arise from the use of that word "natural."

It may appear perfectly natural to set some value on the lives of others and try to save them if you can. "Natural," however, is a word that can be used much too freely. It can be used to provide a supposedly eternal rationale for customs that are merely local and temporary. Asked by Senator Smith for the reason behind the policy of "women and children first," Officer Lightoller replied haughtily that it was "the rule of human nature." Ismay also pronounced it "natural." But that was 1912. At the present time, enforcing the "natural" rule of "women and children first" would get you sued for discrimination. Even in 1912, what was considered "natural" could vary with political ideology. Harried by Senator Smith about the sins of the Marconi Company, one of Ismay's business associates remarked that it was "only human nature" for wireless operators to sell their stories to the newspapers. Smith snapped, "What kind of human nature is that?"[97]

In this connection, it is interesting to notice a book recently published about the *Titanic*.[98] Its author, Steven Biel, is not especially concerned with the rights and wrongs of the disaster itself. He is concerned with what people made of it afterwards. He has therefore compiled the reactions of a multitude of Americans—politicians, preachers, editorialists, feminists, antifeminists, conservatives, socialists, spokesmen for ethnic causes, spokesmen for Americanism—most of whom believed that they had located some deep moral meaning in the event.

These profound, permanent meanings—the kind that one finds in newspapers—often resulted from nothing more than a willingness to ignore fact, abandon logic, and unleash the partisan spirit. Thus, ministers of the gospel denounced Ismay and his corporate associates as exponents of pagan excess, "inhuman monsters who seek to cover their moral deformity with the dazzling splendor of Mammon's throne." Drinking from the same pure spring of self-righteousness, socialists described Ismay as the dreadful "epitome of capitalism," so perfect a product of capitalism that "even capitalism finds it hard to stomach him." To Biel, it seems obvious that the meaning of the disaster grew out of "present circumstances and ideological purposes." It "seared itself into American memory not because it was timeless but because it was timely."[99]

But this is wrong. The *Titanic* story had meaning, and continues to have meaning, because it is a magnificent elaboration, within time, of timeless moral problems.

The problems themselves—involving, as they do, the relationship of duty to danger and of risk to moral responsibility—were not invented in 1912 and are not out of date today. And some of the moral principles that responded to such problems have proven very durable, much more durable, in fact, than the follies, cruelties, and infatuations of popular moralists.

Those moral principles—or, perhaps more properly, moral expectations—expressed an idea of duties and decisions that could not be reduced to risk management. The popular opinion of 1912 doubtless carried this idea to absurd extremes. Captain Smith was regarded as a hero simply because he was apparently willing to go down with his ship. He was celebrated to such a nauseating degree that George Bernard Shaw felt impelled to object; Smith's idolators, he said, had mistaken "sensational misfortune for inspiring achievement."[100] Yes, but there is at least some dignity in deciding that other things may matter besides not being drowned.

Forty-four years after the *Titanic*, when the *Andrea Doria* lay sinking off the New England coast, many crewmen took to the lifeboats and left their terrified passengers behind. This was not a refreshing comment on mid-twentieth-century morality (though it is far from the worst comment that might be cited). Some people tried to cover it up—but no one said it was right.[101] Probably no one would say so today, despite the fact that the action was entirely "natural," in one sense of that word.

But the assumption of moral responsibility is always more artificial than natural. It is the product of choices, often of very hard choices, and not of some purely spontaneous urge. This is the message of the great works of literary art that focus on the problems of moral responsibility, whatever the specific solutions they recommend. These works endure because they reveal, with intensity and rigor, all the possibilities of moral choice. And this thought draws us closer to the permanent significance of the *Titanic*, much closer than we could come by trying to discover whether the particular moral principles invoked on the boat deck of the White Star liner are still alive, or ought to be alive, today.

The *Titanic* has endured because it presented the great problems of morality—which is itself artificial—in the exacting form that one expects from a great work of artifice, a great literary drama. Only in this way could one of 1912's numerous "floating (or sinking) hotels" (in Shaw's words) have transformed itself into an "august event" (in Thomas Hardy's).[102] It was the kind of transformation that one expects from a consummate work of art.

Even while it was happening, the event seemed artificial. A historian of the disaster, summarizing this frequent theme of the *Titanic* literature, describes some features of "the final act of the tragedy":

the great ship lying motionless on a sea as still as a millpond under
the glittering canopy of stars; the rockets soaring aloft into the
darkness from the bridge; the lively ragtime airs played by the
ship's orchestra assembled near the head of the grand staircase; the
passengers standing about in groups, or pacing slowly up and down
in the bitter cold . . . the strange feeling that not a few of them had
of being spectators of a drama rather than actors in it; and all the
time the black water rising higher and higher towards the slanting
decks.[103]

As in a theatre where a production is so brilliantly staged that
the audience cannot suspend its sense of disbelief but continues
conscious of the artistry of sets and human actions, so on the
decks of the *Titanic*. "We had our eyes wide open and noticed
everything that was going on," said third-class passenger August
Wennerstrom, a Swedish emigrant, "but could not feel any sor-
row—or even fear. It was more like we were part of an audience
in a wonderful, dramatic play."[104]

The cast was enormous, yet not so enormous as to prevent
its members from becoming known as individuals. The sets were
perfect complements of the action—magnificent in size yet intri-
cately scaled to the dimensions appropriate to each scene of
individual choice. Ever changing, ever more physically confin-
ing, they closed certain options, while suggesting others; they
required, ever more urgently, that decisions be made, but they
did not determine what the decisions would be. The choices
that each character faced were complex, demanding. Each person had to choose; but this was an intellectual drama, not a
mere thriller. The characters could reflect on their choices (or
not reflect, if that was their way of choosing). The *Titanic* sank
in two hours and 40 minutes, the length of a classic play.[105] The
obvious contrast is with the sinking of the *Lusitania*, when
action was compressed into a mere 18 minutes. Like the
Titanic, the *Lusitania* provided plenty of grist for "ideological"
mills. She would be remembered chiefly as a political incident.
The *Titanic* would be remembered, more richly, as a drama of
her passengers' moral decisions, even when the nature of those

decisions would be hotly debated or abjectly misunderstood. And the dramatic intensity of the *Titanic* infused all the events that surrounded it: the deliberations in the lifeboats, the contrasting choices of the *Carpathia* and the *Californian*, and the enormous re-creations of the whole cycle of events, as staged by the American and British investigators—spectators with their own decisions to make.

Like any great, enduring play, the *Titanic* has spawned a host of critics. To criticize the performance properly, however, one must understand that the performers were not just actors; they were quite capable of being critics, too, and inspectors of their own actions. Often they thought of themselves primarily as spectators. But these spectators were not idle; they had important decisions to make, decisions about right and wrong. It has been argued, indeed, that a sense of morality depends on an essentially theatrical sense of self-observation, a sense that allows one to become, as Adam Smith supposed, a critical "spectator" of one's own performance.[106] The feeling of self-awareness, the feeling that surrounds people who are looking at themselves intently, is common in survivors' versions of the *Titanic* story.

Self-inspection sometimes took a ready, seemingly inevitable course. Jack Thayer, the 17-year-old son of the Second Vice-President of the Pennsylvania Railroad, got separated from his father and mother while passing through a "milling crowd" in the first-class area of the ship, then wandered about the decks until the last boat had gone. He stood on the boat deck with a friend, exchanging messages to be taken back home by whoever might be saved. And "at times we were just thoughtful and quiet":

> So many thoughts passed so quickly through my mind! I thought of all the good times I had had, and of all the future pleasures I would never enjoy; of my Father and Mother; of my Sisters and Brother. I looked at myself as though from some far-off place. I sincerely pitied myself.[107]

No one would question Jack Thayer's sincerity or quarrel with his sympathy for himself in the role he was playing. The actor, looking at himself as though from some far-off place, is often the best judge of his own performance. Another passenger, Masabumi Hosono, would discover this in a very unfortunate way. Hosono was returning from a European trip undertaken on behalf of the Japanese transportation ministry. When the *Titanic* started to sink, he prepared himself to die, if he had to, without disgracing himself in any way. But he wanted to live. When a lifeboat seat became available, he took it, and eventually he arrived back in Japan—only to discover that he had become confused in people's minds with some other Asian traveler who was reputed to have disgraced himself. Hosono, who knew what had happened on the decks of the *Titanic*, and who knew he was innocent, was ostracized nonetheless.[108]

In certain other episodes of the *Titanic* story, as we have seen, the performances were far from the best, and the performers were far from their own most perceptive critics. Some of their choices failed all the common tests of moral criticism; they could be justified only by evasion or absurd rationalization. (Such choices and justifications also have their dramatic interest.) But many performances satisfied the most rigorous demands that could be made by the internal spectator.

These performances were sometimes carried on with solemnity, sometimes with cheerfulness or stoic frankness. During the loading of the lifeboats, Lightoller saw a young couple walking "steadily up and down the deck"; he wistfully imagined that they were on their honeymoon. In the scene that followed, all the actors knew how to play their parts. The "young chap" dutifully offered to help the crew, and Lightoller (as it appears) dutifully declined the offer, refusing to separate him from his bride. As for "the girl—she was little more," she "never made the slightest attempt to come towards the boats, much less to be taken on board, although I looked towards her several times with a sort of silent invitation, but no, she was not going to be parted from her man."[109]

From time to time, Lightoller ran over from the lifeboats to peer into the long emergency staircase that came up from C deck, three stories below. He used the depth of water on the stairs to estimate how much time was left:

> By now the fore deck was below the surface. That cold, green water, crawling its ghostly way up that staircase, was a sight that stamped itself indelibly on my memory. Step by step, it made its way up, covering the electric lights . . . It had now become apparent that the ship was doomed, and in consequence I began to load the boats to the utmost capacity that I dared.[110]

The sets were shifting; the choices were becoming more serious. Characters and points of view were multiplying, as people who would normally have nothing to do with one another were drawn together as actors and spectators, making decisions and watching other people make their own.

That was the context in which Lightoller encountered old Mr. and Mrs. Straus, who had come to the boat deck to make sure that their maid, Ellen Bird, got into one of the early lifeboats. They put Miss Bird into boat No. 8. Alfred Crawford, steward, and Thomas Jones, seaman, were assisting with that boat. Jones saw

> an old lady there and an old gentleman, and she would not come in the boat.
>
> **Senator Francis Newlands [Democrat, Nevada]:** Had she got in the boat?
>
> **Mr. Jones:** No; she would not come near the boat.
>
> **Senator Newlands:** What did she say?
>
> **Mr. Jones:** She never said anything. If she said anything we could not hear it because the steam was blowing so and making such a noise.
>
> **Senator Newlands:** There was a great deal of noise?
>
> **Mr. Jones:** Oh, yes.[111]

But Crawford heard Ida Straus tell her maid "to get into the boat and she would follow her"; he saw Mrs. Straus step "on to the boat, on to the gunwales"—and then he saw her going back

24. Isidor and Ida Straus: A Bavarian immigrant, Straus worked as a young
Southerner for the Confederate government. Later he became co-owner of
Macy's department store, a bank director, a Congressman (one term was
enough for him), an advocate of the gold standard, and an energetic
philanthropist. *Courtesy of the Mariners' Museum, Newport News, Virginia.*

to her husband. He thought "she altered her mind and went back." But perhaps her decision had already been made; perhaps when she walked over to the boat, she was just playing a part to help Miss Bird decide to save herself. Crawford could not have been sure about that. But he caught what Mrs. Straus said to her husband: "We have been living together for many years, and where you go I go."[112]

The Strauses became the still point of a disintegrating world. When Lightoller found them, they were

> leaning up against the deck house, chatting quite cheerily. I stopped and asked Mrs. Strauss [sic], "Can I take you along to the boats?" She replied, "I think I'll stay here for the present." Mr. Strauss, calling her by her Christian name said, smilingly, "Why don't you go along with him, dear?" She just smiled, and said, "No, not yet." I left them, and they went down together.[113]

We know the Strauses by name; we do not know the names of the young couple whom Lightoller found sitting on one of the fan casings on the deck. "I asked the girl, 'Won't you let me put you in one of the boats?' She replied with a frank smile, 'Not on your life.'" (She was "evidently," Lightoller thought, "from the Western States.") "'We started together,'" she said, "'and if need be, we'll finish together.'"[114] Probably they did.

Only two lifeboats could be seen from the after end of the the starboard side when stoker Frederick Barrett came up to A deck. Third-class passengers were waiting to board a lifeboat that had been lowered to that level: "The men stood all in one line . . . as if at attention waiting for an order to get into the boat." When asked who was keeping them in order, he said that no one was; there was no officer needed.[115]

While the *Titanic*'s passengers found their way to the boat deck, her engineers kept working deep inside her, trying to keep her electricity on and her pumps in operation. They did so, until the very end. All of these men perished. The ship's musicians kept on playing, hoping to calm the passengers. None of the band survived.[116]

25. "A night and a day I have been in the deep": Colonel Archibald Gracie went down with the *Titanic,* then managed to swim to Collapsible B. On his return to America, he immersed himself in research on the *Titanic* stories of other people. After reliving the event countless times, he died in December, 1912, a victim, as his family thought, of shock sustained in the disaster. His last words were, "We must get them all into the boats." *Courtesy of the Mariners' Museum, Newport News, Virginia.*

Soon after the iceberg struck, Assistant Surgeon J. Edward Simpson looked up stewardess May Sloan and told her there was mail floating in the hold: "Things were pretty bad." Then he took May and another woman to his room and gave them some whiskey. When May said that she wasn't afraid, Dr. Simpson replied, "Well spoken like a true Ulster girl." Then, May said, "he had to hurry away to see if there was anyone hurt. I never saw him again."[117]

Colonel Gracie, who made it his business to help otherwise unassisted women into the lifeboats, rushed Caroline Brown and Edith Evans toward Collapsible D, the last boat that the *Titanic* launched. Crewmen took the two ladies out of Gracie's hands and started to hurry them into the boat. Miss Evans, who understood the gravity of the situation, insisted that Mrs. Brown get in before her: "'You go first,' she said. 'You are married and have children.'" But when it came Miss Evans's turn, she could not manage to get in; no one knows why. She bravely called out, "Never mind . . . I will go on a later boat." "She then ran away," Gracie says, "and was not seen again."[118]

During the last minutes of *Titanic*'s life, John Jacob Astor helped his pregnant wife into lifeboat No. 4; then, it seems, he hurried to the dog kennels and let Kitty, his Airedale, out for a few moments of freedom on deck. In these final scenes of his life, Astor is said to have delivered the night's most provocative comment on the artificial nature of the prevailing moral code. Standing on the port side of the ship, where people chose to interpret the rule of "women and children first" with special strictness, Astor put a woman's hat on a ten-year old boy and remarked sarcastically, "Now he's a girl and he can go." The boy went in No. 4 and was saved. Astor died in the collapse of a nearby funnel.[119]

Thomas Andrews, an executive of Harland and Wolff, was one of the principal builders of the *Titanic*. He traveled on her maiden voyage so that he could find out what needed to be fixed, and fix it. Nothing was good enough for Andrews; he was a perfectionist. When the collision occurred, he immediately determined that his ship had no chance to survive. He went

26. Thomas Andrews: A leading figure in the construction of the *Titanic*,
Andrews traveled on her maiden voyage to inspect her performance.
He knew how seriously the ship was damaged and did his best to help the
passengers escape, without causing a panic. Andrews decided not to save
himself. *Courtesy of the Mariners' Museum, Newport News, Virginia.*

around the decks trying to make sure that the passengers in all
classes and the women in the crew got into lifebelts and into
boats. Finally, he went to the first-class smoking room and
waited by himself, without his lifebelt.[120]

Meanwhile, writer and editor W.T. Stead, who had published
stories about liners running into icebergs and running out of

27. Benjamin Guggenheim: A businessman and "playboy," Guggenheim took the *Titanic* back from Europe so that he could celebrate his daughter's ninth birthday. *Courtesy of the Mariners' Museum, Newport News, Virginia.*

lifeboats, settled down by himself to read a book. He would die doing what he thought was important.[121]

These were all superb performances, whether they were meant to assist others or only, at last, to assert the actors' sense of themselves. Were they only performances? Perhaps. But if so, the roles selected were appropriate to a moral drama, a drama about what it is right to choose, performed for the actors' moral satisfaction. This is something other than a "social drama" or drama of social forces.[122] It is a drama of people who made individual decisions, often strange and mysterious ones, the dynamics of which can never be truly known.

So important is evidence of a sense of *moral* drama that we are willing to honor it even when we are baffled by the particular code of values that seems to be involved. When the *Titanic* got into trouble, Benjamin Guggenheim and his secretary Victor Giglio went on deck in sweaters and lifebelts. They helped at the boats. Then they took off their belts and sweaters and appeared in evening clothes. "We've dressed up in our best," Guggenheim said, "and are prepared to go down like gentlemen."[123] We may not honor, or even understand, the code of moral dignity, of responsibility to oneself, that Guggenheim thought was embodied in his evening clothes. But we can respect his decision to live up to it.

E Y E W I T N E S S   T E S T I M O N Y

"Prepared to Meet Their Fate"

Testimony of Colonel Archibald Gracie

During this day [Sunday, April 14] I saw much of Mr. and Mrs. Isidor Straus. In fact, from the very beginning to the end of our trip on the *Titanic*, we had been together several times each day.

I was with them on the deck the day we left Southampton and witnessed that ominous accident to the American liner, *New York*, lying at her pier, when the displacement of water by the movement of our gigantic ship caused a suction which pulled the smaller ship from her moorings and nearly caused a collision. At the time of this, Mr. Straus was telling me that it seemed only a few years back that he had taken passage on this same ship, the *New York*, on her maiden trip and when she was spoken of as the "last word in shipbuilding." He then called the attention of his wife and myself to the progress that had since been made, by comparison of the two ships then lying side by side.

During our daily talks thereafter, he related much of special interest concerning incidents in his remarkable career, beginning with his early manhood in Georgia when, with the Confederate Government Commissioners, as an agent for the purchase of supplies, he ran the blockade of Europe. His friendship with President Cleveland, and how the latter had honored him, were among the topics of daily conversation that interested me most. . . .

I recall how Mr. and Mrs. Straus were particularly happy about noon time on this same day in anticipation of communicating by wireless telegraphy with their son and his wife on their way to Europe on board the passing ship *Amerika*. Some time before six o'clock, full of contentment, they told me of the message of greeting received in reply. This last good-bye to their loved ones must have been a consoling thought when the end came a few hours thereafter. . . .

. . . About forty-five minutes had now elapsed since the collision when Captain Smith's orders were transmitted to the crew to lower the lifeboats, loaded with women and children first. The self-abnegation of Mr. and Mrs. Isidor Straus here shone forth heroically when she promptly and emphatically exclaimed: "No! I will not be separated from my husband; as we have lived, so will we die together;" and when he, too, declined the assistance proffered on my earnest solicitation that, because of his age and helplessness, exception should be made and he be allowed to accompany his wife in the boat. "No!" he said, "I do not wish any distinction in my favor which is not granted to others."

As near as I can recall them these were the words which they addressed to me. They expressed themselves as fully prepared to die, and calmly sat down in steamer chairs on the glass-enclosed Deck A, prepared to meet their fate. Further entreaties to make them change their decision were of no avail. Later they moved to the Boat Deck above, accompanying Mrs. Straus's maid, who entered a life boat.

The Truth about the "Titanic," 9–11, 25

E Y E W I T N E S S   T E S T I M O N Y

"That Is All There Was to It"

Testimony of Second Officer
Charles Lightoller

Mr. Lightoller: The purser—as a matter of fact, both the pursers—and the pursers' assistants, of whom I believe there were four—two pursers and four assistants, and two doctors, were there [when the ship was sinking]. Both pursers I was very friendly with, and knew them both intimately, ashore and afloat. They were both thoroughly capable men. . . .

Shortly before the vessel sank I met a purser, Mr. McElroy, Mr. Barker, Dr. O'Laughlin and Dr. Simpson, and the four assistants. They were just coming from the direction of the bridge. They were evidently just keeping out of everybody's way. They were keeping away from the crowd so as not to interfere with the loading of the boats. McElroy, if I remember, was walking along with his hands in his pockets. The purser's assistant was coming behind with the ship's bag, showing that all detail work had been attended to. I think one of them had a roll of papers under his arm, showing that they had been attending to their detail work. . . .

They were perfectly quiet. They came up to me and just shook hands and said, "Good-bye, old man." We said good-bye to each other, and that is all there was to it.

Senator Fletcher: Did any of them get in boats?

Mr. Lightoller: No, sir.

Senator Fletcher: Did any of them survive?

Mr. Lightoller: No, not one.

American Inquiry, 444–45

"He Was Never the Same Again"

The moral drama of the *Titanic* has always had the capacity to transform and intensify people's impression of themselves as "actors" or "spectators."

In 1953, during the production of the film *Titanic*, Barbara Stanwyck was lowered in a lifeboat down the side of a giant *Titanic* model into a water tank. She knew it was a model, and she knew it was a water tank. But when "she caught a glance up at those left behind to 'die' with the ship, she burst into a flood of uncontrollable tears. She said everything had suddenly seemed so real."[124]

A few years later, another *Titanic* film was made: *A Night to Remember* (1958). Lawrence Beesley, who had survived the actual *Titanic* and had written a book about it in 1912, was hired as a consultant. In his book, he had described the moment when the first distress rocket went up over the deck, "with a sea of faces upturned to watch it," and he had said that it was simply "no use denying the dramatic intensity of the scene." Now, having joined the sea of faces watching the disaster happen at the film studio, he was moved to decide that this time he should be among the passengers who did not survive. Sad to say, he was not a member of the actors' union. So he forged a pass, boarded the *"Titanic,"* and stood with the extras who were preparing to

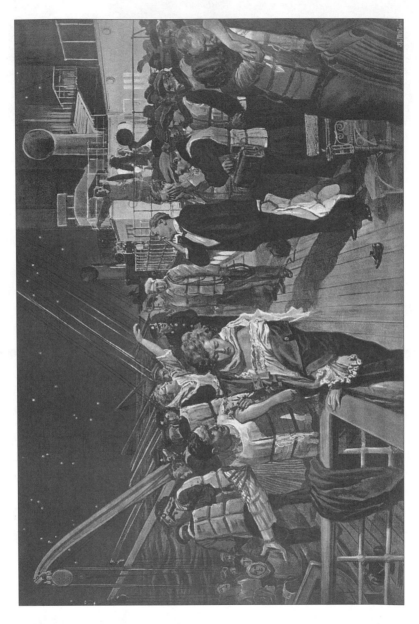

28. Choices on
the boat deck
(lithograph after
Fortunino
Matania, 1912):
An appropriately
theatrical
rendering of the
Titanic's moral
drama.
*Courtesy of the
Mariners'
Museum,
Newport News,
Virginia.*

"die." But "right at the last minute, as the cameras were due to roll, the director spotted [him] . . . Picking up his megaphone, he instructed the amateur imposter kindly to disembark." Beesley's effort to explore "an alternative version of history" had failed.[125]

But what shall we say of Bruce Ismay's alternatives, the various parts he might have played in the *Titanic* story?

He might have performed a starring role, at least in the popular imagination, if he had acted as the captain of industry that Senator Smith expected to see, the kind of man who seizes control of events and can be held directly accountable for the consequences. But Ismay did not see himself as that kind of man. He was a corporate bureaucrat with a justifiably limited idea of his own power.

Ismay might also have had a starring role if he had given his life in an attempt to find other passengers for Collapsible C. The attempt might have been futile. In any event, he did not make it. He did not hold, with his antagonist Mr. Clement Edwards, that he "owed [his] life to every other person on that ship."[126] It is hard to find any definite reason why he should have.

Ismay might have played a still more interesting role if he had chosen to demonstrate, purely for his own satisfaction, a heroic fortitude in the face of death. He could have performed this part only if he had taken a certain highly personal view of the dramatic possibilities of his life; it was not something for public opinion, or a congressional committee, to decide. Ismay did not take that view. He did the work that was immediately at hand; he did it bravely; then he left in Collapsible C.

The dramatic possibilities of the role that he did assume are real enough, but some subtlety is required to appreciate them. Subtlety is completely lost whenever the mysteries of human choices are transformed into myths designed for unreflective minds. In the Nazi propaganda film *Titanic* (1943), the ship hits an iceberg because Ismay, the villainous capitalist, demands that she set a speed record.[127] *A Night to Remember,* the class-conscious British film, presents a series of scenes in which determined efforts are made to keep steerage passengers from reaching the boat deck; then it shows Mr. Ismay shamefacedly entering Collapsible C, beneath the contemptuous stare of the attending officer.

In *Titanic*, a CBS television melodrama (1996), a crowd surges around Collapsible C; a father from third class, denied entrance, is torn, screaming, from his family; then Ismay sneaks out of the shadows and claims his illicit place in the boat, while fellow passengers loudly protest. The musical version of the *Titanic* story that opened on Broadway in April, 1997, features a character named "J. Bruce Ismay" who (as described in one of its advertisements) "pushed Captain Smith relentlessly to set speed records," then "quietly boarded one of the lifeboats while the crew remained behind." [128]

The biggest of all *Titanic* productions debuted in late 1997. The Paramount film *Titanic* risks none of its gargantuan investment on close study of actual personalities. Preoccupied as it is with the romantic adventures of its two invented heroes, it has little use for such a peculiarly actual person as J. Bruce Ismay. He fares better than Officer Murdoch, who is gratuitously charged with taking money in exchange for a lifeboat seat, but Ismay too is flattened and hammered into a paltry shape. He is turned into a publicity hound who bullies Captain Smith into making the *Titanic* go faster so that she (the largest ship in the world) can attract attention from the press. This "Ismay" is a robot who always fulfills his role as one. Even while being told that the ship is filling with water, he asks, "When can we get under way, damn it?"

The young heroine, of course, is on to Ismay from the beginning. She knows that his pride in the *Titanic* is simply a robot's mindless arrogance. When he emits an observation to the effect that the *Titanic* is, indeed, titanic, she puts him in his place by mentioning what Freud has to say about male fixations with "size." This comment figures as an act of courage, quite unlike Mr. Ismay's later defection in the lifeboat, which is presented briefly and routinely, as a shameful but obligatory part of the *Titanic* rite. We see Ismay's moment of sneaking cowardice; we see the attending officer's eloquent pause when he finds him in the boat; we cannot mistake the meaning: the coded images announce that there is nothing more to know.

These are dramas that not even Senator Smith would applaud.

The real J. Bruce Ismay lived out his life at his home in London and his fishing retreat in Ireland, never venturing again on the North Atlantic. The House of Morgan considered him an embarrassment and forced him to retire from his father's steamship line. He continued to serve on the boards of other companies; his favorite company was a railroad. He did not discuss his role in the *Titanic* story; he did not discuss the *Titanic*; his wife thought discussion of that topic would be bad for him. But the historian of the White Star line, who knew Ismay's wife, assures us that because of the way the story had been told by others,

> he was never the same again. He had always been very shy, so much so that few people on board the *Titanic* knew who he was. For once he had come out of his shell, and working with the crew, had done all he could to assist in getting the passengers into the boats. So he was heartbroken to come home to face all the calumny of the Press and public. . . . [129]

His wife gave parties, but he did not attend. He liked to read his business papers on a park bench, where he enjoyed talking to people who were down on their luck; he gave them advice and money, but he never told them who he was. He liked to stand in the crowd to watch parades. He sometimes went to afternoon concerts, where he "always took two seats, the second one for his hat and coat." [130]

When Bruce Ismay entered Collapsible C, he thought that he had made the right choice. When he reached the *Carpathia*, he was shattered by doubts. Subjected to the pressures of public criticism, his resolve strengthened; he decided again that he was right. But we will never know what shapes were assumed by the *Titanic* story (which can never cease to be told) as Ismay repeated it in his own mind, silently and mysteriously, until he died—the victim of a stroke—25 years after the sea closed over the last physical remains of the *Titanic*.

29. The ship and the story: *Titanic* as she was, and (as a story) is today—carefully constructed, elaborately embellished, almost (notice the tugboats and the smoke) ready to encounter the ocean. *Courtesy of the Mariners' Museum, Newport News, Virginia.*

Notes

1. T.S. Eliot, "Burnt Norton," in *Four Quartets.*
2. Walt Whitman, "Passage to India," "Song for All Seas, All Ships."
3. Wilton J. Oldham, *The Ismay Line: The White Star Line, and the Ismay Family Story* (Liverpool: The Journal of Commerce, 1961) 68, 109–110.
4. Oldham 64–65, 136–37, 163.
5. Oldham 137, 136.
6. Thomas E. Bonsall, *Titanic: The Story of the Great White Star Line Trio: The "Olympic," the "Titanic," and the "Britannic"* (Baltimore: Bookman Publishing, 1987) 57–58, 52–55; Wyn Craig Wade, *The Titanic: End of a Dream* (Harmondsworth, England: Penguin, 1979) 449.
7. On the launch, see John P. Eaton and Charles A. Haas, *Titanic: Destination Disaster: The Legends and the Reality,* rev. ed. (New York: Norton, 1996) 58–59. The most convenient source of *Titanic* dimensions and statistics is the Report of the British investigation of the disaster, *Shipping Casualties (Loss of the Steamship "Titanic.") Report of a Formal Investigation into the circumstances* . . . (London: H.M. Stationery Office, 1912), hereafter abbreviated BR.
8. Samuel Hocking, letter of April 11, 1912, in Donald Hyslop, et al., *Titanic Voices: Memories from the Fateful Voyage* (New York: St. Martin's Press, 1997) 114.
9. Wade 49.
10. A spectator quoted in Wade 40; Thomas Hardy, "The Convergence of the Twain."
11. One passenger, Charlotte Collyer, thought that the sudden rush of the *New York* for the *Titanic* "did not frighten any one, as it only seemed to prove how powerful the Titanic was" (Collyer, "How I Was Saved from the Titanic," *Washington Post,* semi-monthly magazine section, [May 26, 1912] 3). Mrs. Collyer's husband Harvey would die in the *Titanic* disaster.
12. One principal source for my account of Ismay's actions on April 10–15

is "the American inquiry" (abbreviated AI): *"Titanic" Disaster: Hearing before a Subcommittee of the Committee on Commerce, United States Senate, 62nd Congress, 2nd Session,* April 19–May 25, 1912 (Washington: Government Printing Office, 1912): testimony of J. Bruce Ismay, 3–5, 7, 11, 13, 17, 915–19, 928, 931–35; Joseph Boxhall, 246–47; Henry Etches, 784–85; Archibald Gracie, 957; Charles Lightoller, 57–58, 430–31; Harold Lowe, 389–390, 401; Herbert Pitman, 276–77; George Rowe, 519–524; and A.H. Weikman, 1095. The other principal source is "the British inquiry" (BI): *Proceedings . . . on a Formal Investigation Ordered by the Board of Trade into the Loss of the S.S. "Titanic",* May 2–July 3, 1912 (London: H.M. Stationery Office, 1912): testimony of Ismay, 437–443, 450, 456, 463–64; Edward Brown, 233, 235; and Rowe, 419–420. (I use the "preliminary" or first daily printings of testimony in the British and American inquiries. When page numbers in later printings are seen to vary in BI, subtract about 6 pp. from every 100 pp. of my citations; in AI, add 32 pp. to pp. 655–972, but from p. 1005 to p. 1145 add 1 p. for every 20–25 pp. of my citations.) Times for the lowering of lifeboats are fairly well approximated in BR 38.

13. Mrs. Lines recalled the overheard conversation in testimony delivered 18 months later, during liability litigation. Her information was not reported to either the American or the British inquiries that convened immediately after the sinking. Her testimony is supplied by George Behe, *Titanic: Safety, Speed and Sacrifice* (Polo IL: Transportation Trails, 1997) 22–24. See also Don Lynch and Ken Marschall, *Titanic: An Illustrated History* (New York: Hyperion, 1992) 41. Behe (16, 25–26) and Lynch (74) summarize some less explicit remarks of Ismay's that Mrs. Emily Ryerson, testifying on the same occasion as Mrs. Lines, remembered hearing in a conversation she had with Ismay at sundown on April 14. From what Ismay said, Mrs. Ryerson gathered that *Titanic* would arrive "very late Tuesday night or early Wednesday morning." The incident does not appear in Mrs. Ryerson's sworn affidavit for the American inquiry (AI 1102–1104). That, of course, doesn't mean her story isn't true. Nevertheless, one wonders how much a maiden-voyage victory over another White Star ship would be worth to White Star itself. Charles Lightoller, *Titanic*'s Second Officer and admittedly not the least favorable witness so far as White Star was concerned, was asked at the American inquiry whether he had heard "anybody discuss" an early arrival time. "No," he replied, "we figured to get in Wednesday morning. There was no object in getting there any earlier" (AI 446–47). If there was an object, it was not the kind that would override normal concern for the survival of the ship. Third Officer Pitman (AI 302) took a Wednesday arrival for granted and thought there wasn't enough coal to go much faster. It has never been shown that Ismay gave Captain Smith advice about navigational issues; e.g., taking chances with speed in icefields.

14. Compare Gracie's testimony at the American inquiry (AI 957) with his book, *The Truth about the "Titanic"* (New York: Mitchell Kennerley, 1913) 16–17.

15. Lawrence Beesley, *The Loss of the S.S. Titanic: Its Story and Its Lessons* (Boston: Houghton Mifflin, 1912) 79–80.

16. See Gracie's contemporary estimate of the population (300). He says 27 women and children, basing his figure largely on Rowe's evidence, which is definite and sensible but because of a problem in addition yields either 43 or 39 people, total (AI 520, BI 419-20). Gracie gets one crewman in the wrong boat (compare Weikman, AI 1095). I discount the strange testimony of Hugh Woolner, who suddenly remembered that, by the way, he had helped to quell a mob at Collapsible C (AI 854), about 20 minutes after that boat was actually launched; and Jack Thayer's recollections, written many years later and filled with confusions, in which he pictures Ismay "push[ing] his way into" a lifeboat (Thayer, *The Sinking of the S.S. Titanic* [1940; Chicago: Academy Chicago, 1998] 341). Both accounts are cited by Walter Lord, *The Night Lives On* (New York: William Morrow, 1986) 128–29. (Might Woolner, who more than once quite confidently confuses times or places, have witnessed some scene of violence elsewhere among the boats?) I also discount an unconfirmed rumor related by Charles Lightoller about Ismay's having been "bundled" into Collapsible C by Chief Officer Henry Wilde, who allegedly assured him that there were "no more women on board" (AI 429). This story is supported by ship's barber Weikman (AI 1095) but put in doubt by quartermaster Rowe (AI 521). Ismay may have confided the story to Lightoller and Weikman, and to his sister-in-law (see Oldham 216–17), and it may be true; but Wilde, who did not survive, could not vouch for its accuracy, so Ismay may have decided not to risk it in public. As to Collapsible C's "stowaways," who were discovered, by Rowe's account (AI 520), only "when daylight broke," they probably benefited from other passengers' tacit permission to escape in this way. Lifeboats are large, but not that large.

17. The *Titanic* struck the ice on her starboard side and at first listed in that direction, but as water filled spaces of various shapes within the hull, she developed a list to port.

18. Ismay AI 17, AI 929; Lightoller, AI 426; Arthur Rostron, marconigram, cited at AI 1123; Oldham 195–96. Feeling responsible for the butler and secretary, Ismay provided their widows, as Oldham says, with a generous lifetime annuity.

19. Wade 74; *New York Times* (April 21, 1912) 2.

20. A.T. Mahan, in Gracie 321–23; Brooks Adams, in Wade 375.

21. Wade 156–57.

22. My discussion of Senator Smith relies for its facts on the long and very sympathetic account in Wade. On the Taft connection, see esp. Wade 146. On the Harter Act, see esp. 196–97, 221, 362. Wade's respect for Smith is shared by many other *Titanic* people. Eaton and Haas (107) even mention Smith's "objectivity."

23. Ismay, AI 3.

24. Ismay, Texas, did change. Ismay, Montana, which had been named in honor of May and Isabel Earling, daughters of a railroad president, heroically resisted—until 1993, when it renamed itself Joe, Montana, in honor of Joe Montana. See Lord, *The Night Lives On* 212–13; and Jonathan Raban, "The Unlamented West," *New Yorker* (May 20, 1996) 61, 66.

25. Wade 368–69. Wade doesn't call this envy. He treats it as righteous political indignation.

26. Guglielmo Marconi, AI 484–85, 817, 493–94; William Alden Smith, AI 841.

27. Wade 165–66, 183, 195–96; Ismay, AI 930.

28. Wade 429.

29. Lord, *The Night Lives On* 206–210.

30. Ismay, AI 927; Wade, 449; Harold Sanderson, BI 471. For the scope of the *Olympic*'s remodeling, see "White Star Liner 'Olympic.' Structural Alterations," *The Marine Engineer and Naval Architect* 35 (May, 1913) 382–83.

31. Sir Rufus Isaacs, BI 900; Sir Robert Finlay, BI 850.

32. John Charles Bigham, Baron Mersey, BI 759.

33. Mersey, W.D. Harbinson, BI 624.

34. Mersey, BI 490.

35. Ismay, BI 440.

36. Ismay, BI 452, 443, 453. Why *had* people lingered below decks? The usual answers, and true enough, involve lack of awareness that the ship was actually going down, a desire not to leave baggage behind, the complexity of some routes to the boat deck, confusion about where these routes began, isolated attempts by crewmen to keep third-class passengers in third-class areas, and the general failure of officers to organize evacuation of the lower regions. Daniel Allen Butler, *"Unsinkable": The Full Story of RMS "Titanic"* (Mechanicsburg PA: Stackpole Books, 1998) 105, 106, adds American immigration laws requiring physical separation of the third class.

37. Ismay, BI 464.

38. A. Clement Edwards, BI 785; Mersey, BI 799; Finlay, BI 809.

39. BR 40.

40. Wade 442.

41. Robin Gardiner and Dan van der Vat, *The Titanic Conspiracy: Cover-Ups and Mysteries of the World's Most Famous Sea Disaster* (Secaucus NJ: Citadel Press, 1998) 28. The authors regard Ismay as "a weak character" who was "dazzled" by the "rapacious" J.P. Morgan's "wealth and power" (54). Plutocrats might do almost anything, or so the authors seem to think. They give serious consideration to the fabulous theory that the vessel that sank in the North Atlantic on April 15, 1912, wasn't the *Titanic* at all; it was really the *Olympic*, which after being damaged in a collision with the cruiser *Hawke* in September, 1911, was purportedly switched with the *Titanic*. The *Olympic*'s corporate owners, so the theory goes, might have decided to rid themselves of damaged goods by transposing the name plates of the two sister ships. This would allow the company to send one *"Titanic"* roaring off into an ice field, sink her, and pick up the insurance money, while retaining another *Titanic* (now, of course, named *Olympic*) for use in making still more money (98–99, 260–61). The authors finally drop this "substitution theory," but they retain their conviction that the *Titanic* "died of wilful negligence" (262).

42. Alfred Crawford, AI 810; Alfred Olliver, AI 528.

43. Isaacs, BI 580.

44. Edward Wilding, BI 517–18.

45. On *Pacific* and other victims of ice, see Wade 56–57; on *Naronic*, see Oldham 122–24.

46. Lightoller, BI 306–307.

47. Frederick Passow, BI 572; Isaacs, BI 669.

48. Finlay, BI 850; Isaacs, BI 903; Mersey, BI 907.

49. Gary Cooper, *The Man Who Sank the Titanic?: The Life and Times of Captain Edward J. Smith* (Stoke-on-Trent: Witan, 1992) 59; Eaton and Haas 77. The figure of £1,000, mentioned by Cooper (58), would be a substantial increment to Smith's salary of £1,250. In today's money, £1,000 would have the buying power of something like $75,000.

50. Bonsall 46. Bonsall (36–37, 46, 48) gives a good summary of Smith's mysterious behavior and discusses the panic explanation.

51. Edward Brown, BI 234.

52. Gracie, 114–323, establishes the port-starboard disparity in exhaustive detail. Even on the port side, however, some males had to be invited into boats because they were needed to manage them.

53. Mr. Roche, BI 772. Here there is also the suggestion, which helps the boats for all argument (see chapter 5), that if there had been lifeboats for all, there might still have been a rule of preference for women and children, but less time would have been spent in selection of people for each boat, and fewer boats would have been sent away unfilled because of shortness of time. Of course, the very knowledge that boats were in short supply incited some people to work faster, for good or ill.

54. Mersey, BI 543.

55. Frederick Fleet, in Hyslop 162.

56. Bonsall 46.

57. Charles Lightoller, *Titanic and Other Ships* (1935), in *The Story of the Titanic As Told by Its Survivors*, ed. Jack Winocour (New York: Dover, 1960) 288. Lightoller clearly felt the need to defend his reluctance to put as many people as possible into *Titanic*'s boats, but his basic point is sound enough.

58. Des Hickey and Gus Smith, *Seven Days to Disaster: The Sinking of the Lusitania* (New York: Putnam's, 1982) 204–234.

59. "The 'Titanic' Judgment and the Advisory Committee's Report," *The Marine Engineer and Naval Architect* 35 (September, 1912) 35; George W. Hilton, *Eastland: Legacy of the Titanic* (Stanford: Stanford University Press, 1995) 4.

60. Bonsall 54; Violet Jessop, *"Titanic" Survivor*, ed. John Maxtone-Graham (Dobbs Ferry NY: Sheridan House, 1997) 171–180. Though a hospital ship, *Britannic* happened not to be carrying patients; if she had been, as Maxtone-Graham points out (177), her death toll might have surpassed *Titanic*'s.

61. William Hoffer, *Saved! The Story of the "Andrea Doria"—the Greatest Sea Rescue in History* (New York: Summit, 1979).

62. J. Bernard Walker, *An Unsinkable Titanic: Every Ship Its Own Lifeboat* (New York: Dodd, Mead, 1912). The experts at *The Marine Engineer and Naval Architect* ("The 'Titanic' Judgment" 35–36) advanced similar views.

63. Isaacs, Mersey, BI 596.

64. Lightoller 305.

65. Information on the regulatory and Great Lakes situations is derived from Hilton 5–13.

66. Hilton 75–112, 137.

67. Curiously, Mersey's recommendation of the new requirement of boats for all has failed to mollify critics who see his investigation as an attempt to "sanitize" such matters as the lifeboat requirements under which the *Titanic* sailed (see Lynch 182).

68. Ismay, AI 16; Wilding, BI 514; Mersey, BI 855.

69. Isaacs, BI 658; Finlay, Mersey, BI 855.

70. Mersey, BI 835.

71. BR 30.

72. Mersey, BI 835.

73. Edwards, BI 796. The same question is asked by Walter Lord, *The Night Lives On* (165–191), and Wade (338–61), who provide useful introductions to the *Californian* episode. On Captain Lord's statements about whether the *Titanic* was visible from his location, what the rockets were, and the log, see AI 685–86, 696–97; BI 161–62, 168–169. Much *Titanic* speculation centers on the *Californian* and its identity or lack of identity with the "mystery ship" sighted by Olaus Abelseth (see his testimony above, p. 55) and other people. On the *Californian* and its captain, see the pro-Lordite Leslie Harrison, *A Titanic Myth: The "Californian" Incident*, second ed., rev. (Hanley Swan, Worcs.: The S.P.A. Ltd., 1992), and the anti-Lordite Leslie Reade, *The Ship that Stood Still: The Californian and Her Mysterious Role in the Titanic Disaster*, ed. Edward P. De Groot (New York: Norton, 1993).

74. Isaacs, BI 957–58. Reade, 101–103, takes a similar view.

75. Lightoller 294.

76. Reginald Lee, BI 75.

77. Charles Joughin, BI 142–45; Walter Lord, *A Night to Remember*, rev. ed. (New York: Holt, 1976) 151–52, 170.

78. Harold Bride, *New York Times* (April 19, 1912) 1–2; AI 1050, BI 388. For the three-minute interval, see BR 41, 67. This figure, based on calculations too complex to summarize, could be increased by, say, two minutes, depending on one's judgment of the speed of sinking.

79. Emily Ryerson, AI 1104; for timing: Walter Perkis, AI 582.

80. Lowe, AI 409–410. It is fair to mention that Lowe, of whom Daisy Minahan (see pp. 103–104, above) was so critical, was always quite prepared to save people who might appear at the edge of the crowd.

81. Frank Evans, AI 677-78; Edward Buley, AI 605.

82. Lowe, AI 410.

83. Collyer 13. In true period style, Gracie lists the young man as "a plucky Japanese" (154). Collyer's account is partially corroborated by that of George Crowe, a steward who told the American inquiry that "a Japanese or Chinese young fellow" was "picked up on top of some of the wreckage—it might have been a sideboard or table—that was floating around" (AI 616). Lowe said to Senator Smith, "I do not know who these three live persons

were; they never came near me afterwards, either to say this, that, or the other. But one died, and that was a Mr. Hoyt, of New York" (AI 408). It is one of the *Titanic*'s mysteries that neither witnesses nor investigators at the two inquiries ever really wanted to discuss the Asian survivors (whose precise national identity is ordinarily left to guesswork). This was a time in American history when ethnic hatred was easily roused, and the press was not above rousing it. The morally alien Mr. Ismay appeared in newsprint as a man of "distinctly Oriental" features (Wade 160); the *New York Times* had no compunction about rushing into print with accounts of "Chinese stokers piling into the bottom of the boats before the women could clamber in, and attempting violently in at least one instance to wrest away and even cut from off one passenger the lifejacket he had put around him" (*New York Times* [April 19, 1912] 2, 3.) When *Titanic* witnesses and investigators avoided discussion of Asian passengers, they may have been trying *not* to stir up passions; they may have wanted to let the Asian travelers, immigrants, or "stowaways" (see note 16, above) make good their escape with as little publicity as possible. If so, this is yet another indication of the intricacy of moral response that one finds in almost every scene of the *Titanic* drama.

84. Crawford, BI 429–30; Lynch 144; Hyslop 164.

85. Henry Etches, AI 786; Olliver, AI 529–530; Alfred Shiers, BI 114; Pitman, Smith, AI 283–84.

86. Robert Hitchins, Mersey, BI 48; Frederick Fleet, AI 366; Arthur Peuchen, AI 338; Margaret Brown, in Gracie 134–39.

87. C.E.H. Stengel, quoted in United Press dispatches to the *Vancouver World* (April 19, 1912) 26, 28; Stengel, AI 948, 940.

88. Lucy, Lady Duff Gordon, *Discretions and Indiscretions* (New York: Stokes, 1932) 163–64. The author, who informs us that she can hardly bear to tell this "story of horror unparalleled in the annals of the sea" (162), apparently had the assistance of journalistic sources in recalling some of the less plausible details.

89. Stengel, AI 945, 946–47.

90. Sir Cosmo Duff Gordon, BI 284, 288, 278.

91. Charles Hendrickson, Mersey, BI 119, 121.

92. Mersey, George Symons, BI 258.

93. Thomas Scanlan, Albert Horswill, Mersey, BI 274–75.

94. Mersey, Robert Pusey, BI 295.

95. Mersey, BI 285; Edwards, Duff Gordon, BI 286.

96. Duff Gordon, letter of [August] 25, [1912], reproduced in Hyslop 198.

97. Lightoller, AI 88; Ismay, AI 9; P.A.S. Franklin, Smith, AI 672.

98. Steven Biel, *Down with the Old Canoe: A Cultural History of the "Titanic" Disaster* (New York: Norton, 1996).

99. Biel 72, 128, 132.

100. George Bernard Shaw, London *Daily News*, May 22, 1912; in Shaw, *Agitations: Letters to the Press 1875–1950*, ed. Dan H. Lawrence and James Rambeau (New York: Ungar, 1985) 149.

101. Hoffer, esp. 135–39, 208–209.

102. Shaw 148; Hardy, "Convergence of the Twain."

103. Geoffrey Marcus, *The Maiden Voyage* (New York: Viking, 1969) 150.

104. August Wennerstrom, in Wade 299. And Wennerstrom may not have been in the best mood to appreciate the dramatic quality of the occasion. Not only had the *Titanic* placed him in imminent danger of death, but he had even had difficulty getting himself into that situation. He is described as a radical journalist (real name, August Andersson) who had made himself notorious by calling the king of Sweden the "king of thieves" and who needed to purchase false papers in order to leave the country ("Passengers on the *Titanic*," *Swedish Press* 63 [May 1991] 21).

105. Like many other writers, Biel (156–160) recognizes the appeal of this dramatic situation, but he prefers to attribute it to Cold War nostalgia for an age that offered "time to die" instead of instant death in atomic warfare. One wonders whether this theory also applies to *King Lear.*

106. Adam Smith, *The Theory of Moral Sentiments* (1759).

107. Thayer, 343. Thayer jumped from the ship, found overturned collapsible lifeboat B, spent a harrowing night on it, and found his mother when he reached *Carpathia*. His father was lost, as was the friend with whom he spent his last minutes on the ship. In the excitement, he seems to have forgotten the messages exchanged (compare Thayer's account in Gracie 222).

108. Joseph Coleman, "Titanic Account from Sole Japanese Survivor Sheds Light on Disaster," Associated Press report, Tokyo, December 19, 1997.

109. Lightoller 292.

110. Lightoller 291.

111. Gracie 142; Francis Newlands, Thomas Jones, AI 571.

112. Crawford, AI 112, BI 429. One can hear an allusion (theatrical, in the best sense) to the book of Ruth: "Whither thou goest, I will go" (1.16). Gracie's evidence (25) is that the decision had already been made.

113. Lightoller 293.

114. Lightoller 293.

115. Frederick Barrett, BI 69.

116. Isaacs, BI 930.

117. May Sloan, letter of April 27, 1912, in Jessop viii.

118. Gracie 37–39.

119. The story about Kitty is reconstructed from Mrs. Astor's memories by Eaton and Haas, 23. The story about the little boy (William Carter Jr., whose father had left some time before in Collapsible C), is doubtfully told by Lord, *Night to Remember* 173, less doubtfully by Butler, 135–36. The hat would have belonged to Billy's mother; the comment would be about right for Astor.

120. Butler 43; Weikman, AI 1095; Lord, *Night to Remember* 77–78, 86–87, 111.

121. Lord, *Night to Remember* 103–104.

122. As Biel (8) considers it.

123. Etches, *New York Times* (April 20, 1912) 9.

124. Cooper 156.

125. Julian Barnes, *A History of the World in 10½ Chapters* (London: Cape, 1989) 173–74; Beesley 79. In his book, Beesley develops a curious view of the disaster as a whole. He argues (A) that the *Titanic* was the world's "safest ship"; (B) that she succumbed to a "one-in-a-million accident"; (C) that everybody is morally responsible for such accidents, because everybody shares "the immorality of indifference"; and (D) that "the remedy" for this universal sin is legislation, by which "the possibility of such a disaster occurring again [will be] utterly removed" (Beesley 4, 233, 240, 248–49, 254–55). The conclusion is similar to Senator Smith's, but the logic is much more mysterious.

126. Edwards, BI 453.

127. Paul Heyer, *"Titanic" Legacy: Disaster as Media Event and Myth* (Westport CT: Praeger, 1995) 126.

128. *New York Times* (February 9, 1997) H14.

129. Oldham 216, 220–24, 232; quotation 217.

130. Oldham 229–230.

Bibliography

The *Titanic* Story in Other Books

Of the making of books about the *Titanic* there is no end. We have reached the point where a good book could be written about all the other *Titanic* books (all the books to date, at least). What choices of evidence, approach, and style shape their versions of the story? What risks, literary or intellectual, do the authors run? Why do they write these books, anyway? What happens to them as a result? A book could be written about these subjects—but this book isn't it. What follows is simply a selection of some basic works, and some that are significant in other ways, with a bit of critical commentary. Omission of any book does not imply its lack of interest. Favorable notice of any book does not imply acceptance of its specific assumptions and conclusions.

I. The Great Inquiries

The records of testimony given at the British and American investigations of the *Titanic* disaster are the most extensive sources of information about that event. They are documents essential to any serious study of the subject. But they are more than that. Together, they constitute one of the most absorbing chapters in the book of human life. Like any other great and various work, they demand to be read in their entirety, and from start to finish, with no skipping of seemingly "technical" or otherwise "unimportant" passages. Seeing the parts enables one to see the whole, and in this case both the whole and the parts are well worth seeing.

Board of Trade, United Kingdom. *Proceedings . . . on a Formal Investigation Ordered by the Board of Trade into the Loss of the S.S. "Titanic."* London: H.M. Stationery Office, 1912.

Committee on Commerce, United States Senate. *"Titanic" Disaster: Hearing before a Subcommittee of the Committee on Commerce, United States Senate, 62nd Congress, 2nd Session.* Washington: Government Printing Office, 1912.

Both inquiries were first printed in daily installments, then reprinted as a whole (also in 1912) but with pagination that can vary from that of the daily pamphlets. Both inquiries were reprinted in 1998 in fairly expensive editions, the first by the British Public Record Office (Kew, Surrey), the second by the Congressional Information Service (Bethesda MD). A paperback edition of the American testimony ("extensively excerpted," with a short, cliché-scarred introduction) appeared in the same year: *The Titanic Disaster Hearings,* ed. Tom Kuntz (New York: Pocket Books, 1998).

Records of evidence given in the inquiries are not to be confused with the comparatively brief, though valuable, reports that resulted; as follows:

[John Charles Bigham, Lord Mersey.] *Shipping Casualties (Loss of the Steamship "Titanic.") Report of a Formal Investigation into the circumstances . . .* London: H.M. Stationery Office, 1912.

Reprint: *Report on the Loss of the S.S. Titanic.* New York: St. Martin's Press, 1990.

Another reprint of the report is included with the 1998 Public Record Office reprint of the British *Proceedings,* where confusion is created by the use of *Shipping Casualties . . . Report of a Formal Investigation . . .* as the title of the whole.

Committee on Commerce, United States Senate. [Senator William Alden Smith.] *"Titanic" Disaster: Report of the Committee on Commerce, United States Senate . . . Together with Speeches Thereon by Senator William Alden Smith of Michigan and Senator Isidor Rayner of Maryland.* Washington: Government Printing Office, 1912.

The great majority of the American report is reprinted in *The Titanic Disaster Hearings,* ed. Kuntz.

II. Works of History and Interpretation

Ballard, Robert D., with Rick Archbold; illustrations of the *Titanic* by Ken Marschall. *The Discovery of the Titanic.* New York: Warner-Madison Press, 1987.

A well-written, well-illustrated account of Ballard's 1985 and 1986 expeditions to the *Titanic*'s wreckage.

Beesley, Lawrence. *The Loss of the S.S. Titanic: Its Story and Its Lessons.* Boston: Houghton Mifflin, 1912.

Reprinted in Winocour, below. Beesley, an observant man, was a second-class passenger on the *Titanic*, and he got right to work turning his observations into a book. This is generally thought to be the best written of the survivors' narratives, and it is, although Beesley's murky thoughts about risks and regulations (see note 125, above) constitute a substantial literary debit.

Behe, George. *Titanic: Safety, Speed and Sacrifice.* Polo IL: Transportation Trails, 1997.

An admirably clear and straightforward argument for the guilt of Ismay and the White Star line. Behe suggests that Ismay and the *Titanic*'s officers tried to beat the time of *Olympic*'s maiden voyage, thereby inviting disaster; that *Titanic*'s deck officers ignored actual sightings of icebergs in the hour before the crash; and that Ismay and White Star deliberately covered up the evidence of their responsibility for the disaster. Behe offers an excellent summary of the anti-Ismay, anti-White Star evidence (such as the recollections of Mrs. Lines [see note 13, above]). Unfortunately, the evidence consists largely of more or less distant recollections, third-hand stories, and old-fashioned yarns, toward all of which Behe is too hospitable.

Biel, Steven. *Down with the Old Canoe: A Cultural History of the "Titanic" Disaster.* New York: Norton, 1996.

Academic writers seldom want anything to do with the *Titanic*, perhaps because they regard an interest in good stories as embarrassingly naive (especially if the stories are true). Biel, an academic, at least makes a close approach to the subject. But what really rouses his interest is not the *Titanic* per se but the ideas (mostly inane) that contemporary people formed about the disaster while under the influence of their social and political biases. His critical account of these notions is "cultural" in one academic sense of the term but not especially illuminating. His research demonstrates the astonishing fact that early-twentieth-century America was marked by inequalities, conflicts, and anxieties, and that this kind of thing can affect people's perceptions of world events.

Bonsall, Thomas E. *Titanic: The Story of the Great White Star Line Trio: The "Olympic," the "Titanic" and the "Britannic."* Baltimore: Bookman Publishing, 1987.

A concise illustrated history of *Titanic* and her sister ships, with fine pictures and genuinely informative text and captions. Bonsall's analysis of the *Titanic* disaster is brief but penetrating.

Bride, Harold. "Thrilling Tale by Titanic's Surviving Wireless Man as told in *New York Times,* April 28, 1912." In Winocour (below).

It *is* thrilling. The story resulted, by the way, from one of those paid interviews that so greatly upset Senator Smith (see pp. 23, 25, above).

Butler, Daniel Allen. *"Unsinkable": The Full Story of RMS "Titanic."* Mechanicsburg PA: Stackpole Books, 1998.

No one can actually write the full story, but Butler manages to write a lot of it. His generalizations about the historical context are often just that, generalizations, and too strongly marked by stereotypes; but his account of the central event is fresh and vivid. He is outspokenly opposed to the interference with historical writing of "latter-day moralizing, social leveling, mythmaking, or finger pointing," and that is all to the good.

Cooper, Gary. *The Man Who Sank the Titanic?: The Life and Times of Captain Edward J. Smith.* Stoke-on-Trent: Witan, 1992.

Records of the *life,* especially the internal life, of Captain Smith are insufficient for a full-scale biography, so Cooper tries to finish as much of the portrait as he can by painting in the background of Smith's *times.* He supplies valuable information about the environment of Smith's youth, about the experiences of British merchant seamen, and about what might be called the externals of Smith's own career on shipboard. This information does contribute to the portrait, but the central figure remains elusive—no fault of Cooper's.

Eaton, John P., and Charles A. Haas. *Titanic: Destination Disaster: The Legends and the Reality*. Rev. ed. New York: Norton, 1996.

Many evocative pictures and a lucid, fact-filled narrative, provided by two of the foremost experts in the field.

————. *Titanic: Triumph and Tragedy*. Second ed. New York: Norton, 1995.

Another data-rich retelling of the story, with illlustrations—not necessarily beautiful ones, but of significant documentary value.

Gardiner, Robin, and Dan van der Vat. *The Titanic Conspiracy: Cover-Ups and Mysteries of the World's Most Famous Sea Disaster*. Secaucus NJ: Citadel Press, 1998.

The authors fail to find a conspiracy, though they try hard enough (see note 41, above). While trying, they run across many pungent facts about both the *Titanic* and the *Olympic*.

Gracie, Archibald. *The Truth about the "Titanic."* New York: Mitchell Kennerley, 1913.

Reprinted as *Titanic* (Chicago: Academy Chicago, 1986); as *Titanic: A Survivor's Story*, in the same volume with John B. Thayer, *The Sinking of the S.S. Titanic* (Chicago: Academy Chicago, 1998); and in Winocour (below.)
  The title of this book does not signify any attempt to be sensational; Colonel Gracie is simply imitating the title of his earlier book, *The Truth about Chickamauga*. Gracie is nobody's idea of an entertaining writer, but he was a dedicated researcher. Not content with relating his own experiences, which involved swimming for his life from the *Titanic*'s wreck, he tracked down all the information he could find about everyone else's. His account of what went on in each lifeboat provided a framework for future investigations of an important subject; it stands up pretty well today. A book of fundamental importance.

Harrison, Leslie. *A Titanic Myth: The "Californian" Incident*. Second ed., rev. Hanley Swan, Worcs.: The S.P.A. Ltd., 1992.

Most *Titanic* researchers believe that the ship's distress rockets were visible from the liner *Californian*, which had halted for the night some miles away; and that the captain of that vessel, Stanley

Lord, knew about these rockets and culpably neglected to make a responsible investigation of their meaning. Some researchers believe that the *Californian* was actually the "mystery ship" whose lights were sighted from the *Titanic* and her lifeboats. Other researchers doubt some or all of this; and some of them determinedly defend Captain Lord from all aspersions. *Titanic* studies have been characterized by a protracted conflict between "Lordite" defenders and "anti-Lordite" accusers, with significant displays of knowledge and ingenuity (not to mention venom) on each side. People who are seriously interested in the *Titanic* ought to acquaint themselves with the complexities of both sets of arguments; in the process, they will learn a good deal about ships and the people who have to do with them, and about the risks of human judgment. Harrison's book is one of the many possible places to start reading about the *Californian*. He is a principal defender of Captain Lord. (See also Padfield and Reade.)

Heyer, Paul. *"Titanic" Legacy: Disaster as Media Event and Myth.* Westport CT: Praeger, 1995.

Heyer presents much useful information about the *Titanic*'s adventures in the seas of radio, press, and cinema. The book is clearly and unpretentiously written but becomes somewhat tiresome when it touches on "technological hubris," "our disregard for nature," and similar themes.

Hilton, George W. *Eastland: Legacy of the Titanic.* Stanford: Stanford University Press, 1995.

The definitive account of the disastrous capsizing of the Great Lakes steamer *Eastland* in 1915. Hilton argues that a crucial factor was the extra lifesaving equipment loaded on the *Eastland* as a result of the post-*Titanic* boats-for-all movement. "The *Titanic* disaster," he maintains, with much supporting evidence, "provoked a thoroughly erroneous evaluation of the risks of sea travel." The book says little about *Titanic* herself but a lot about maritime risks and regulations. It is a judicious and well-documented work of scholarship, and its account of the *Eastland* disaster is gripping.

Hyslop, Donald, Alastair Forsyth, Sheila Jemima. *Titanic Voices: Memories from the Fateful Voyage.* New York: St. Martin's Press, 1997.

A collection of pictures, interviews, and documents, with connecting historical narrative, focused on the *Titanic*'s relationships with

Southampton, the port from which she sailed. The pictures are often beautiful and are generally of historical importance; the interviews and documents are sometimes noteworthy, sometimes not; the editorial work is not the finest.

Jessop, Violet. *"Titanic" Survivor.* Ed. John Maxtone-Graham. Dobbs Ferry NY: Sheridan House, 1997.

The posthumously published memoirs of a woman who was a crewmember on all three *Olympic*-class liners and survived the destruction of two of them. Jessop is intelligent and personable; she takes some poetic license with the facts, but she offers lively pictures of ships as they are known by the people who make them work. Maxtone-Graham, a good editor, appreciates his author, finds and corrects her errors, and supplies pertinent information about her subjects. His introduction places her experience in the context of the nineteenth and twentieth centuries' remarkable progress in rendering travel across the Atlantic noticeably more agreeable than a voyage to hell.

Lord, Walter. *A Night to Remember.* Rev. ed. New York: Holt, 1976.

First published in 1955, *A Night to Remember* remains by far the most popular *Titanic* book, and deservedly so. It is the history of the disaster, told in an unpretentiously vivid style. Lord has a fine sense for the resonant detail and the memorable anecdote, and he knows how to build them into a swift and powerful narrative. He succumbs neither to sentimentality nor to idle speculation; and although he seldom pauses for detailed analysis of events or their implications, he is clearly the master of his evidence. More than four decades later, he is rarely found to have made a mistake. The 1976 edition makes minor corrections in the text and adds fine and copious illustrations.

———. *The Night Lives On.* New York: William Morrow, 1986.

This sequel to *A Night to Remember* is an engaging analysis of a number of special issues, such as officers' gunshots, what the band was playing, what happened to various survivors, and the *Californian* affair.

Lynch, Don, and Ken Marschall. *Titanic: An Illustrated History.* Toronto: Hyperion-Madison Press, 1992.

A very beautifully produced, large-format book. Marschall provides impressive original illustrations (there are also many fine period photographs), and Lynch provides a fast-paced retelling of the tale. The book's treatment of the British inquiry is surprisingly one-sided and hostile.

Marcus, Geoffrey. *The Maiden Voyage.* New York: Viking, 1969.

A general history of the *Titanic* that gives special attention to sea-faring matters and to the two post-disaster inquiries. Its attitude is generally skeptical toward the public professional judgments of those involved.

O'Donnell, E.E. *The Last Days of the Titanic: Photographs and Mementos of the Tragic Maiden Voyage.* Dublin: Wolfhound Press; Niwot CO: Roberts Rinehart Publishers, 1997.

Frank Browne, later Father Frank Browne, an important Irish photographer who knew ships and liked them, traveled on the *Titanic* from Southampton to Queenstown. It was a sort of holiday. He took pictures, which he later published and (by adding *Titanic* pictures taken by other people) made into an album. This is all of historical and human interest; some of the pictures are also of aesthetic interest. The elaborately and lucidly edited volume includes explanations of the images and biographical information on Father Browne.

Oldham, Wilton J. *The Ismay Line: The White Star Line, and the Ismay Family Story.* Liverpool: The Journal of Commerce, 1961.

Serves up masses of information, leaving the reader to digest it as well as possible. Some very telling indications of the Ismays' personalities can be found amid the quotations and summaries of documents.

Padfield, Peter. *The "Titanic" and the "Californian."* New York: John Day, 1965.

A significant defense of Captain Lord of the *Californian.* (See also Harrison and Reade.)

Pellegrino, Charles. *Her Name, Titanic: The Untold Story of the Sinking and Finding of the Unsinkable Ship.* New York: McGraw-Hill, 1988.

An account of the *Titanic*'s sinking, of Robert Ballard's expeditions to the ship's remains, and of the author's sentiments about these things. Tediously over-written and impressionistic, with the occasional bright idea.

Quinn, Paul J. *Titanic at Two A.M.: Final Events Surrounding the Doomed Liner.* Saco ME: Fantail, 1997.

A good idea for a book, somewhat marred in execution, *Titanic at Two* is an elaborate recreation of the ship's final minutes, with both narrative and illustrations by the author (additionally, there are good period photographs). Quinn's speculations are sometimes insufficiently grounded, and the book would inspire more confidence if it recognized the "special place" of evidence from the British as well as the American inquiry. But its treatment of most issues (even the *Californian* problem) is crisp and clear.

Reade, Leslie. *The Ship that Stood Still: The Californian and Her Mysterious Role in the Titanic Disaster.* Ed. and updated by Edward P. De Groot. New York: Norton, 1993.

A massive assault on Captain Lord of the *Californian* and the arguments advanced in support of him. From the literary point of view (at least), this is a classic work among *Titanic* books. It is the investigation of a seemingly minor mystery (what did Lord do, and why did he do it?), performed in the grand style—abundant in argument, patient in pursuit of fact, superbly ironic, acute in its insights into human problems: a book that makes its conclusions hard to resist. (See also Harrison and Padfield.)

Thayer, John B. *The Sinking of the S.S. Titanic.* Chicago: Academy Chicago, 1998. Published in the same volume with Gracie, *Titanic: A Survivor's Story* (see Gracie, above).

Jack Thayer was 17 years old when he survived the *Titanic*; he was 28 years older when he published this account of the disaster for the information of his family. Although his memory is sometimes demonstrably wrong, his account of his experience deserves to be read.

Wade, Wyn Craig. *The Titanic: End of a Dream.* Harmondsworth, England: Penguin, 1979.

The most important book on the story of the *Titanic* as it emerged from the American Congressional investigation led by Senator William Alden Smith. An excellent researcher, Wade draws information from many sources, including Smith's papers, contemporary press accounts, and of course, the testimony given at the American inquiry; and he forms it all into a coherent account of the investigative process. This is an important service to scholarship—though it would be still more useful if Wade had provided specific documentation of his facts, not just a list of sources at the end. (Lack of specific documentation is disappointingly common among *Titanic* books, even those that are admirably researched.) The book's other defects are its foggy view of historical conditions (in 1912, we learn, "luxury and excess were justified on assumptions of limitlessness, both in fuel and in human suffering") and its sentimental regard for the greatness of Senator Smith.

Winocour, Jack, ed. *The Story of the Titanic As Told by Its Survivors.* New York: Dover, 1960.

Includes Beesley's and Gracie's books, the chapters about the *Titanic* from Officer Charles Lightoller's *Titanic and Other Ships* (1935), and wireless operator Harold Bride's story as published in the *New York Times* (April 28, 1912).

Index